Felix Publishing 2020
email: info.felixpublishing@gm.
Print copies available from publisher.

A Pocketbook for Hiking and Survival

2020 Print Edition   ISBN: 978-1-925662-32-0
digital book release ISBN: 978-1-925662-33-7

Author: Dr. Peter T. Scott
Illustrations by the author

Registration:
Thorpe-Bowker +61 3 8517 8342
email: bowkerlink@thorpe.com.au

A Pocketbook for
Hiking and Survival

Peter T. Scott

Introduction

This is a guidebook to survival in the field. It is not extensive, as does not cover all terrains nor all climates but is designed for the average person who decides to go into the wild and wishes to have some tips about living there for a short time. It is meant to be used as a reference in the field, not in the library!

Some parts of this book contain sections to be filled in before a trip. Use a pencil for all such information as many inks run when wet. Erase the specific information when the trip has been completed.

With an electronic copy of this book, ensure that the device is waterproof and is fully charged (solar-powered chargers are can be purchased as a good backup)

Personal Details

In case of an emergency:

NAME:

_____

DATE OF BIRTH: /   /

RELIGION: _____

HOME ADDRESS:

_____

_____

TELEPHONE:(_____) _____

                  Mobile: _____

CURRENTLY STAYING AT:

_____

_____

Telephone:-(_____)_____

NEXT-OF-KIN:
(Relationship)_____

(Name)_____

(Address)_____

_____

(Telephone)(_____) _____

                  Mobile: _____

Medical Details

BLOOD TYPE: _____

KNOWN ALLERGIES & REACTIONS TO MEDICINES:_____

_____

DISABILITIES/CURRENT MEDICATION:

_____

_____

MY DOCTOR:

(Name)_____

(Address)_____

(Telephone:)(_____)_____

    Mobile: _____

LOCAL AMBULANCE/POLICE/RESCUE:

(at)_____

(Telephone:) (_____) _____

    Mobile: _____

    Radio Call sign/Frequency (e.g. marine channel 16)

    _____

HEALTH INSURANCE:

Company:_____

(Number/Code)_____(Telephone)

Emergency Numbers

Many countries use common numbers for emergencies. Assuming that the mobile phone is working, the following numbers may be tried. Language may be a problem.

Countries		Alternatives
Africa (most)	**112**	117, 999, 122
Asia	**112**	911, 999, 119, 113
Australia	**000**	112 for mobiles
Americas	**911**	110, Brazil 190, Chile 133, Columbia 123, Cuba 106
Europe	**112**	France 17, Greece 100, Russia/Ukraine 102, Hungary 107, Poland 997,
Pacific	**911**	112, 999

Other Details

_____

_____

_____

_____

_____

Table of Contents

Chapter One: Before the Trip

Thorough planning prevents discomfort and the chances of an accident.

Make copies of the trip information (below) and give it to a reliable person (e.g. local Ranger, Police Officer, Club Official, etc.) **before** the trip and **notify this person when all members of the party have returned.**

1.1 Objectives & Trip Details
PURPOSES OF THE TRIP:

1._____

2._____

3._____

4._____

WHERE ARE YOU GOING? (Name, Location/map name & grid references. – give a sketch map or plan of any local variation to map)

_____

_____

_____

_____

_____

_____

Map Sketch:

HOW ARE YOU GETTING THERE?
(Transport, General Route, Camps etc.)

_____

_____

_____

_____

TIMINGS:
Date/Time of Departure:

_____

Departing From:

_____

Estimated Date/Time of Arrival (Main or first
camp)_____
Send Help After (Time/Date):

_____

1.2 People in the Group

WHO IS IN THE GROUP? (Total Number: Names, Addresses, Contact Numbers)

_____

_____

_____

_____

_____

_____

_____

_____

_____

_____

_____

_____

_____

_____

_____

_____

_____

_____

1.3 Checklist

(Use a pencil to check each item once done). Some trips will not require all of the items listed and other trips may require specialized gear. Details about certain basic items are given in later Chapters.

For EACH person, check:

- TRIP DETAILS GIVEN TO SAFETY PERSON(S)   [ ]
- TRANSPORT ORGANIZED   [ ]
- BOOKING & FEES PAID   [ ]
- FITNESS CHECK   [ ]
- BASIC SHELTER such as:
  - Tent -lightweight   [ ]
  - Tent fly or over cover   [ ]
  - Tent pegs (enough + spares)   [ ]
  - Tent poles -lightweight telescopic   [ ]
  - Ropes for tent + 10 m spare   [ ]

- GROUNDSHEET (also as spare cover) e.g. large clear   [ ]
  plastic.
- GROUNDSHEET (orange plastic – in emergencies can   [ ]
  be cut into two panels for attracting attention)
- SLEEPING GEAR such as:
  - Sleeping Bag (cold weather type)   [ ]
  - Inner blanket (e.g. woolen sheet folded over)   [ ]
  - Mattress (e.g. thin foam, air bed, light-weight   [ ]
    stretcher or hammock + rope)
- LIGHT & HEATING such as:
  - Small stove (e.g. alcohol, small gas, hexamine/'fire   [ ]
    starters'
  - Fuel container/bottle - tight seal   [ ]
  - Waterproof matches – tight box   [ ]
  - Small head lamp + spare cells   [ ]
  - Candles (4 / week)   [ ]
  - Small length of rubber tire inner tube to start a fire   [ ]
    in rain

- CLOTHING such as: [ ]
  - Trousers (long, strong)   [ ]
  - Trousers (spare)   [ ]
  - Shirt (long-sleeve, cotton 2 - pocket)   [ ]
  - Shirt (Spare, flannel in Winter)   [ ]
  - Underwear or Swimwear (2 pair nylon or cotton)   [ ]
  - Socks (2 pair woolen)   [ ]
  - Hat (broad brim)   [ ]
  - Boots (strong, ankle grip, laced)   [ ]
  - Sandals in plastic bag   [ ]
  - Wet weather gear (e.g. over pants, jacket with hood [ ]
    or cape)
  - Cold Weather Gear – always carry (e.g. thermal   [ ]
    underwear, extra jumper/jacket, gloves, woolen
    Balaklava).

Some areas get very cold, very quickly even in the midst of hot summers.

- WATER depends upon conditions e.g.1 to 4+   [ ]
  litres/day (carry enough for emergencies for 2 days)
- WATER BOTTLES/BAG e.g. strong, flexible style   [ ]
  well-sealed with straps
- STERILIZATION TABLETS or Condy's Crystals   [ ]
- FOOD enough for trip + 2 days emergency. Light   [ ]
  weight. Reduce cans. Dry food if plenty water
  available. Sealed packs. Nutritious.
- UTENSILS such as:
  Strong knife 8-15+ cm blade, Saw edge in belt pouch   [ ]
  with sharpening stone
  Knife-fork-spoon kit   [ ]
  Tin opener (army type on lanyard)   [ ]
  Boiling can (e.g. 'billy')   [ ]

Small frying pan [ ]
Metal plate & Cup [ ]
(There are small, compact kits of full cooking utensils
e.g. Trangia type)
Scourer & small dish towel [ ]
- PERSONAL HYGIENE such as:
  Soap in plastic box [ ]
  Small towel in plastic bag [ ]
  Hand sanitizer – small bottle [ ]
  Face washer [ ]
  Toothpaste & brush in plastic box [ ]
  Razor (as appropriate) [ ]
  Comb or hair brush [ ]
  Toilet paper (roll in plastic bag) [ ]
- SEWING KIT – small, strong thread, large needles, [ ]
  buttons
- FIRST AID KIT small, containing roll bandage, pack [ ]
  sterilized gauze, antiseptic cream/powder, roll
  plaster, paracetamol tablets, salt, scalpel blade, band-
  aids, small lens, tweezers, personal allergy items.
- SUN-BURN CREAM [ ]
- SMALL WHISTLE [ ]
- NAVIGATION EQUIPMENT
  GPS or Cell Phone GPS (Note: many areas are not [ ]
  covered or are in 'dead spots'. GPS units can also be
  damaged easily by heat/water or are dropped and
  lost) Always have back up items and know how to use
  them e.g.
  Compass - liquid filled survey/army [ ]
  Survey map of area – latest, in plastic map cover [ ]
  Aerial photos (often show hazards not on maps so are [ ]
  useful)
  Protractor for map direction angles [ ]

Pencil, eraser (Chinagraph pencils are water proof [ ]
and mark on plastic map covers)
Ruler (may be on protractor)   [ ]
Small notebook and pencils   [ ]
- BACKPACK – good support, waterproof with several [ ]
pockets

Other additional items may include small walkie-talkies if the group is large and may get spread out. These often have low range unless more professional hand-sets are obtained.

The above list may seem a lot but many items have several uses such as the lens in the First Aid Kit is also good for starting a fire or looking for small items on aerial photos.

From experience, these items and food and water for up to four days have been carried by the author in a variety of terrains and climates.

1.4General Advice
1.4.1 Know the Limitations:
- of yourself at your current state of health;
- of members of your party:
One must be aware of their fitness and any health problems and limitations. Never assume that everyone is fit and healthy. Find out.

FIVE is the best minimum for bad country or climate

so that in an accident, two can stay with the injured and two go for help. In safe conditions perhaps three could be OK.

Travelling alone is dangerous, but if required it needs extra care, planning and caution and is not recommended for beginners in rough country;

- of your equipment:

Take nothing for granted. **Check** that all that is needed is present and that everything is in good order and works correctly. Take spare parts & repair kits as needed. Marine or freshwater trips must have all of the necessary safety equipment such as buoyancy vests, flares, anchors, drinking water, paddles and an EPIRB emergency device if at sea.

1.4.2 Know the Country:

- seek and heed local advice about:

terrain(relief/surface);
hazards (natural & man-made);
weather patterns;
water(quality/availability);
roads and tracks(access/surface);
No-go areas (avoid or seek
permission to enter).

- obtain recent local maps of good reliability - aerial photos are also good to have in support. **Don't rely on electronic devices.**
- carefully plan the route. Consider:

distances to travel;
timings;

steepness of land;
type of ground;
type of vegetation;
camp sites;
alternative places to shelter;
watering points;
hazards (rivers, swamps, cliffs,
   thick vegetation etc.);
escape routes in an emergency;
and always prepare a Navigation Data Sheet
before starting the trip.

1.4.3 Prepare for Emergencies:

- every member of the party must know the trip plan and what to do in an emergency (lost or injury). Have an IF LOST plan involving simple movement towards an obvious place (e.g. stream or road or downhill) or, in difficult conditions, staying still and make signals for help;
- at least one person should have basic First Aid training if possible and for a larger group, carry a First Aid Kit and some emergency supplies. Everyone should have an extra day's rations and water and be familiar with the first signs of fatigue, hypothermia and heat stroke in oneself and others and be able to treat these conditions.

1.4.4 Leave Details with local Police, Rangers or other responsible persons stating:

- who is in the party? (number, gender, age);

- where you are going? (route, camps & times);
- estimated return time (and place of return);
- general summary of your experience & equipment.

REMEMBER TO REPORT BACK TO AUTHORITIES UPON RETURNING

Chapter Two: Equipment

2.1 In General

All equipment, both personal and group should be:

- in good working order;
- suitable for the trip (including emergencies);
- minimal for needs;
- as light in weight as possible; and
- able to be simply repaired if damaged;

2.2 Basic Equipment (for each person) should include:

TENT - lightweight with fly, built-in groundsheet and mosquito net. With room for self & gear. A "Three-Person" type gives good room for two people + equipment. The fly (a covering independently stretched over the tent) is important for additional water-proofing and protection from the heat by giving air circulation between it and the tent roof.

Ensure that any tent poles (telescopic, aluminium are best) and tent pegs for both tent and fly are sufficient in number but allow an extra 50% just in case. They must be suitable for the area e.g. use longer and wider pegs for sand and hard-packed snow. Steel pegs are better than weaker aluminium pegs.

Extra rope is always handy and a tight roll of Venetian-blind chord (say 30 m) is always useful. A small roll of

Duct Tape is always handy.

SLEEPING BAG – Lightweight, waterproof & warm. Down (filled with fine feathers) is the best for warmth and are lightweight but they are expensive and tend to lose their insulation properties after being wet as the feathers clump together.

Wet bags can be turned inside-out and hung over dry tree branches or over a line inside a shelter. Care trying to dry them near a fire! After drying, the bag must be thoroughly shaken to spread out the feathers within their separate compartments.

Kapok - filled bags and polyester bags are cheaper and can be restored easily after being wet but older bags are bulky and heavy and are not as good in very cold weather. Most bags come in a plastic or canvas bags for protection, but it is also a good idea to tightly pack (or roll) the bag into a black plastic bag first and then tightly seal the end. Thin garbage-bin liner bags are good for this purpose.

An inner bag can be made from an old flannel blanket folded lengthways and stitched along the bottom and along three-quarters of one side. In cold areas it is better to have extra layers on the inside of the bag and beneath the bag itself (use clothes).

If the climate is warm, then use the bag as a mattress but

ensure that the body is protected against dew and insects.

EXTRA GROUND SHEET (In addition to tent floor) is always handy especially if it is an orange or yellow coloured thin plastic type. Use 3m x 3 m (or longer) as several of these make good emergency signal panels.

An ideal spare ground sheet is of the poncho variety which has a hole and hood for the head and serves as an additional body and pack cover during rain (but protection for the legs is needed). The ex-army 'tents-half shelter' are best as they sometimes come as ponchos and can be used separately as a small tent or two can be clipped together to form a larger tent. Two of these are best for lightweight hiking as they have a variety of uses and can be used as alternatives to full tents, groundsheet and rain protection.

A small, emergency "space-blanket", having an aluminized surface should also be carried as it gives good warmth in emergencies. It can be folded to pocket size but take care near flame!

WATER & CONTAINER(S) - enough water for the entire trip plus two days should be taken. Never rely upon resupply unless permanent good water is certain.

A strong container - strong, light in weight (such as the flexible bag type) which is unlikely to leak is best. Several water bottles on a belt or in a convenient (separate) pouch of the pack will also do. A useful container can be made out of a thoroughly cleaned (and sterilized) four – six litre wine cardboard cask inner which is then carried in a strong canvas bag.

All containers must be filled at home before the trip - do not rely upon local water on the track. If local water is used, it should be sterilized by boiling for a few minutes (use any surplus water after the evening tea/coffee - cover the boiling can and let it cool) or use Water Sterilization Tablets (pack the number appropriate for containers plus refills & emergency).

FOOD - should be high in energy & nutritional value, long-lasting, light in weight, can be carried easily and can easily be prepared under adverse (wet/cold) conditions.

This may include fresh foods such as potatoes, onions, tough peelable fruit, dried foods such as dehydrated vegetables, pasta, rice and dried or preserved meats. Remember that dried foods will require much more water than other foods.

Dried cereals, small tin foods, tea/coffee, sugar, dried or tube condensed milk, salt, flour, curry powder and sugar are also easy to carry.

UTENSILS - should include two metal containers to boil at least one litre of water or more, a small frying pan, a metal drinking mug and a deep plate.

A knife-fork-spoon set, can-opener (Army spoon type on thin lanyard is best) and a good utility pocket knife completes the basics.

There are kits such as the compact Trangia type that contains all of the basics which can be packed into a small bag and then into a side pouch of the pack.

A knife with a good-size and serrated blade which can be carried in a belt pouch with sharpening stone is essential. It should be not less than about 10 cm (4 inches) in length.

A small, metal garden trowel is also useful for digging holes, removing hot coals from the fire and other needs.

All eating utensils must be thoroughly cleaned after use. Some biodegradable detergent (minimal) in a small, screw-capped bottle is useful, although a soap bar can be shredded with a knife. Sand works well for scouring although a small scouring pad can also be wrapped around the detergent bottle and both kept in a sealable plastic bag.
Use a small chamois for drying as they often come in a small sealed pack.

Keep liquid wastes to a minimum and try to carry non-degradable rubbish out of the area to proper bins.

LIGHTING & HEATING - never rely on the local

vegetation as being the only source of light and heat. Lack of natural fuel, wet weather, National Park rules and fire restrictions may prevent the building of the usual camp fire. Always carry a small stove for cooking and some source of waterproof light, preferably as a small headlamp with extra batteries.

There are many types of small, compact camping stove available. These may use solid fuel such as hexamine solid fuel as used in army as personal stoves. 'Fire-starter' solid fuel can easily be purchased in supermarkets. Other small stoves, including those used in the Trangia kits use alcohol, often sold as 'methylated spirits'.

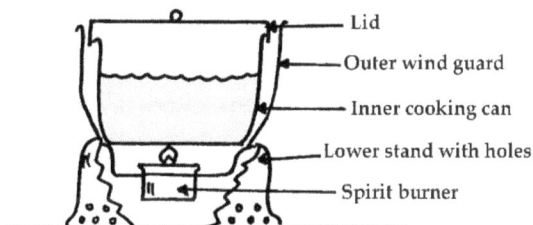

A 'Trangia'-style cooking arrangement

Fuel must be carried in a strong (e.g. metal) bottle with a very good seal. If small butane gas stoves are used, care should be taken when using and disposing of the gas cans.

Waterproof matches and some candles are also useful but care must be taken with candles within or near a tent. A candle stand can be made from an old tin with wet sand in the bottom:

Matches can be protected from damp by waxing them (use melting candles) completely and packing them into a small plastic container (glue the striker onto its lid). A cheap, old-style cigarette lighter with a simple flint wheel is also a handy source of flame and small 'eternal match' consisting of a flint and metal striker can also be purchased.

CLOTHING – should be suitable for the worst possible weather in the area. Never assume that conditions will be normal and mild. Mountainous areas may have snow in Summer and heat wave conditions with fires and lack of water may occur in any part of the country.

Always take wet-weather gear even if conditions have been fine, especially in mountainous regions or where sudden changes of weather are possible. Light nylon over-pants are very handy as well as a waterproof, light-weight but warm padded waterproof jacket. A hooded cap is good in wet weather as it covers the head, body and backpack.

Good, strong clothing which cover arms and legs is best. Tight-fitting or heavy clothing is not recommended and a broad-brimmed hat is necessary for protection from the sun. A woolen cap of the Balaklava type which covers all of the head except the face is useful in cold weather. Good, strong, and comfortable boots with strong ankle support are essential. These should be "worn in" before the trip to prevent blisters and discomfort. Socks should be dry and made from wool. In cold or wet conditions, two pairs of woolen socks being worn at the same time to keep moisture from accumulating and to ensure a good (but not too tight) fit. Light, cotton inner socks may be worn inside woolen socks in hotter weather, but synthetic socks are not recommended.

When unlaced, boots should have enough space behind the heel at the ankle to put in a finger.

Spare underclothes (or swim wear), socks (two pair), long-sleeved shirt, swim trunks and an extra woolen jumper are best carried in a plastic bag folded up inside the sleeping bag which is within a waterproof bag is best. Light shoes or sandals and boot polish with brush can be carried in a separate plastic bag.

TOILET GEAR – may consist of a cake of soap (in container), face washer (in plastic bag), toothpaste & brush (in plastic container), razor (as appropriate) and a small face mirror (useful also for signaling). All can all be held in small bag in a separate pouch of the pack. A small towel or chamois sponge is useful for drying the body.

Toilet Paper is best carried within the pack and in a sealable plastic bag along with a small bottle of hand sanitizer. For larger parties, a "Bush Toilet" or small pit can be dug with a garden trowel. The trowel should be left on the heap of sand near the pit to cover the remains and a roll of toilet paper can be place on an upright forked-stick and covered with an old can or plastic bag. Hand sanitizer should also be hung on the stick. Hygiene should be stressed and practiced in a group trek.

FIRST-AID KIT - everyone should have a personal kit and some knowledge of when and how to use it. More detail about first aid is given in a later chapter. Larger groups should also have a more comprehensive First Aid kit.

RUCKSACK or PACK - This should be of light-weight, water-proof canvas or synthetic cloth with a good aluminium or stainless-steel frame (e.g. "H" type). It must be comfortable to carry with shoulder straps and back pads so that the pack is supported high on the back. For heavy packs good hip supports allow the weight to be taken lower down on the body as well. Exterior pockets are useful provided that they do not bulge too far out from the side.

Loading the pack is very important and some thought should be put into the order that items will be needed. Items that may be needed quickly as in an emergency (e.g. first aid kit) or in a sudden change in weather (e.g. wet or warm weather gear) should be easily accessible without going through the entire pack.
Items such as water, insect & sunburn cream, some food, camera etc. should be packed last, near the top of the pack

or in convenient side pockets. Other items such as sleeping bag, spare clothing, additional food and extra water may be packed at the bottom for use that night. The tent, fly, poles and rope will be packed on top of the pack.

Breakable items should be packed in rigid containers (e.g. eggs can be packed inside the mug with paper). Fine material (e.g. tea, flour, sugar etc.) should be sealed in plastic bags (use re-sealable type) and pushed into spaces between clothes.

Hard objects (e.g. cooking utensils, spade, fuel bottles etc.) should be placed so that they do not rub nor protrude into the body whilst one is walking. Flat objects may be pushed down the inside of the pack at the sides and facing outwards.
When the pack has been finally loaded it should be well-balanced with a low centre of gravity (heavy things in the bottom) and equal weight distribution on either side.

The pack should not be over-loaded and thought should be given to discarding non-essential items. Even for a long walk, the pack should be light enough to allow a comfortable, even walking pace and to be able to be lifted up onto the back easily.

There is a tendency for beginners to pack far too much gear, tinned food and unwanted gadgets. Most of the equipment described so far is light-weight and takes up minimal space. Never take any more than what is absolutely necessary.

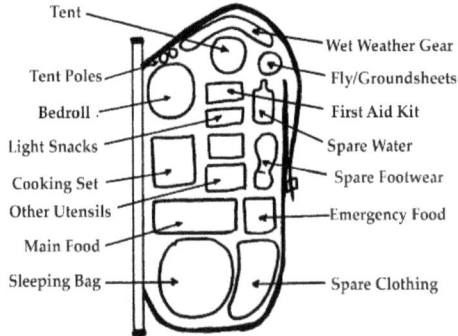

A well-planned pack (side view)

2.3 Navigation Equipment - is essential. Even with a simple track system in a national park, a map showing the tracks is essential.

A GPS units, including some cell phones and watches are extremely useful but for longer walks, a solar charging unit is needed or spare batteries if possible. One should not rely completely on GPS units as they may suffer damage from water or heat and may not operate in some locations. Basic navigation equipment should also be taken as a backup. For most walks, the bare essentials include:

MAPS - of the entire area in which the walk is to be taken. It should be a good map with contours showing elevation, a good scale, legend and reference grid. Survey and Army maps are best. Maps must be up-to-date or be supplemented with recent aerial photos (very useful) or local amendments added.

COMPASS - good fluid-filled variety (not cheap) with clear markings and a strong case. It must able to take bearings along a sight (e.g. prismatic or Sunto type).

PROTRACTOR - to plot bearing on map with sharpened pencil. A clear circular type is adequate. Some come with ruler markings or romers (divisions matching map scales).

MAP CASE - this may be of a simple plastic wallet type to protect the map in wet weather. Chinagraph (oil-based and waterproof) pencils can be used on the outside of the plastic to mark bearings, routes etc.

Ex-Army map cases are good because they have a backing board for firm support and folds for pencils, protractor etc.

2.4 Emergency Kit - in addition to the personal First Aid kit, emergency food and water, and spare clothing for wet or cold conditions, a small kit of useful items should be carried in an accessible pocket. It could probably be in a sealed container that would be carried in the shirt pocket. It should only be used in the case of emergencies and may contain:

- small whistle for signaling or alarm
- 'Space Blanket' (200cm x 127 cm aluminium-coated)
- small mirror (or shiny inside lid)
- matches - waterproofed, held in duct tape with striker card.
- small candle - short length
- small magnifying glass or lens
- needle & strong thread
- small hooks, line & small sinkers
- glucose tablets (as many as possible)
- paracetamol tablets (about 6)
- water sterilizing tablets
- small surgical blade (scalpel -sealed)
- plaster ("Elastoplast")
- condoms - ideal water carriers.

All should fit into a small, sealed (use several turns of duct tape) tin or plastic container. This kit should be carried at ALL TIMES on the person - it is for use when one has been separated from the other items of comfort carried in the pack.

Chapter Three: Water

3.1 General
Water is the most essential survival requirement. One can exist without food for several weeks, but death from dehydration can occur in as little as two or three days.

Water is obtained by the body from drinking, food intake, body conversion of and stored fat. Water is lost by exhalation of breath, sweat, urine, vomit and from passing solid waste.

The amount of water lost depends upon:
- ambient temperature and climate;
- activity;
- medical condition; and
- type of person.

For example, the **daily** rate of water **loss** for an adult is about:
- resting in shade (Temperate areas) 1 litres;
- normal activity and some rest (temperate zones) 2-3 litres;
- sitting in the tropical sun 6 litres;
- walking in the tropics up to 14 litres.

On average, about one litre of fluid per hour is lost during exercise. Extreme heat and humidity can raise that amount to three litres per hour.

Whilst total water content of the human body varies greatly from person to person, the average is about two-thirds of the body weight. Only a small percentage of the body's water needs be lost to cause dramatic effects:

5% loss - may cause thirst, sleeplessness, lack of appetite and flushed skin;
10% loss - difficulty with breathing and walking, headache and dizziness;
20% loss - delirium, swollen tongue, inability to swallow, numb and loose skin, and finally death.

Signs of dehydration include:

- extreme thirst
- headaches
- lethargy
- mood changes and slow responses
- dry nasal passages
- dry or cracked lips
- dark-coloured urine
- weakness
- tiredness
- confusion and hallucinations.

3.2 Amounts of Water Needed
This can vary greatly depending upon the condition, activity and the size, age and body functions of the person. On the average, under normal conditions (moderate temperature, a mixture of activity and rest)

about **3 litres per day** is required just for drinking. This can be reduced with good water control, limited activity and sensible use of foods (cut down on excessively sweet, salty or dried foods) to about two litres per day, but up to six litres per day or more may be needed in hot weather with much activity and using some dried foods.

When planning the trip, consider:
- **potential climatic conditions**, general and local terrain;
- **individual water needs** activity, personal fitness and health requirements. Washing & hygiene;
- **chance of re-supply** - natural water, and the need for sterilization;
- **carrying water** - remember that 1 litre weighs 1 kilogram and how can it be carried comfortably.

Before the trip, individuals and/or the trip leaders needs to estimate the amount of water that needs to be carried. The most recent information about potential water points for resupply should be known.

The following table shows how long a person can last with different amounts of water whilst resting in shade. The amounts in brackets are those with moderate walking (at night):

Survival Times (in days) for Water Needed					
Temp.	Available Water Amount (litres)				
	Nil	1 L	2 L	4 L	10 L
HOT >37C	2-5 (1-3)	2-6 (2-3)	2-6 (2-3)	3-7 (2-4)	3-11 (3-6)
WARM 26C-37C	5-9 (3-7)	6-11 (3-8)	6-12 (3-8)	7-14 (4-10)	11-23 (6-14)
COOL <26C	9-11 (7-8)	11-12 (8-9)	12-13 (8-10)	14-16 (10-12)	23-25 (14-17

3.3 Carrying Water

Water containers can be worn on a sturdy and comfortable belt (e.g. Army canteen in metal "dixies"), be carried internally within a pocket of the pack in rigid, tightly-sealed water bottles or externally in a carry bag hydration system with drinking tube. The most preferred option seems to be several water bottles. A useful home-made alternative is the inner bag of a cardboard wine cask. The silver plastic liner, which will hold 4-6 litres, can be thoroughly cleaned and carried in a protective hessian or canvas bag over the shoulder. Moreover, if the hessian is wet, evaporation also cools the water inside:

Wine cask skin inside

Canvas or Hessian Bag

Spout from cask through a cut-out hole

A "wine cask" water bag

For a day trip in hot weather, a two litre juice bottle can be three-quarters filled the night before and placed in the freezer. The next morning, the frozen bottle is packed into the food bag. This keeps the food cool and provides ice water for most of the day. For day trips this amount seems adequate but if there is a chance of an emergency, extra water should be carried.

For trips more than two-three days long, water re-supply will have to be considered. This can come from natural water supplies (streams, springs etc.) or from designated **pre-arranged** sources (farm houses, tanks, villages, support party caches etc.).

Regardless of the pristine nature of the area, always suspect natural water sources as containing harmful organisms such as bacteria and protozoans, toxic farm wastes or natural poisonous mineral salts, especially in old mining areas.

3.4 Sterilizing Water
In general, do not drink water (even sterilized) which is:
- stagnant and foul-smelling (unless desperate);
- contains dead animals;
- contains blue-green algae;
- contains no life and looks bright green or yellow;
- has a ring of salt or minerals around its edge.

For other waters, if the area seems fresh, there is life in the water and it is **flowing**, the water will probably be safe. To ensure that it is really safe then it can be sterilized by:

- boiling it for a few minutes (with the lid on);
- adding a few crystals of "Condy's Crystals" (Potassium Permanganate) until the water is light pink;
- adding Chlorine-based "Water Sterilizing" tablets which can be obtained from camping shops; or by using
- commercial water filter/purifying containers.

If the water is muddy or has other particles in it, then it can be clarified prior to sterilization by:
- pouring it through a **clean** sock or bag which contains some fine sand, washed charcoal (from the fire) or fresh grass cuttings; or
- placed into a large pot with a handle which is then spun several times around the head.

If the water is so badly contaminated or salty, it will have to be distilled. This can be done by placing the water into a large pot or water can and covering it with a rolled-up absorbent cloth (e.g. clean towel). Boil the water and carefully lift off the hot, sodden cloth with a stick and place it into a dry, cold container to cool. Squeeze the sodden cloth out when cool and repeat the process until sufficient water has been obtained.

Other more elaborate campfire distillation systems could

probably be arranged so that the steam coming from the boiling water is cooled and collected elsewhere. A simple solar distillation system is given later on in this book.

3.5 Finding Water

Water may not be obvious but can be found by looking in the right place or by following some signs. For example:

- **underground water** - can be found in limestone and other caves, outcrops of fractured rock and where the water table (the top surface of water filling pores in rock or soil) comes near or to the surface. Look for springs at the base of cliffs or in gullies and rock crevices or where vegetation is greener. A hole may have to be dug but not if the area has a foul smell.

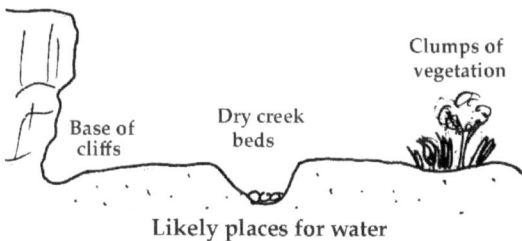

Likely places for water

Near the sea, drinkable water can be obtained by digging a hole about 3 - 6 metres deep into the sand about from the water's edge (at high tide) or by digging in hollows of coastal sand dunes. Sometimes the water table moves up into dune systems giving small lakes of freshwater.

- **animal signs** often indicate water sources. Animals such as wild bees, pigeons and grain-feeding birds such as parrots (galahs and cockatoos are the exception) and ants usually need a daily water supply. Follow them or their trails at the end of the day to locate soaks or water in rock and tree hollows. Make a small mop on the end of a stick to soak up water in tree hollows.
- **collecting dew** - even in deserts, the slight amount of water in the air will condense during the cool early morning as dew which settles on low plants and grass. Tie rags or tuffs of grass around the ankles and walk through the damp grass (wring these out). Shake dew of broad-leaf plants (not those with stinging hairs, or bright red leaves and fruit or those plants with a milky sap). Cacti leaves may have moisture droplets on them in the early morning.
- **extract water from plants** such as thick brown vines in rain forests, shallow roots (especially of mallee scrub, bottle-brush, wattle, baobab, she-oaks) and some thick leaves ("pig-face" and "prickly-pear") and stems of plants like cactus. AVOID plants which have stinging hairs, red parts and give a milky sap.

Cut short lengths (about 30-50 cm.) of the plants using a knife to make an angular cut across the root or stem and stand vertically in a can or pot or in an angled, grooved channel of bark, bamboo, or an envelope of plastic etc.:

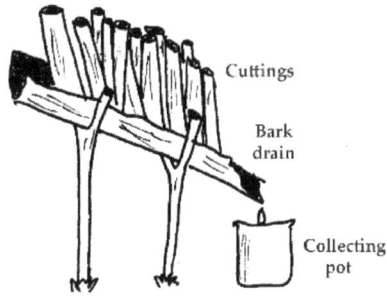

Collecting water from plant cuttings

- **from evaporation from the soil and impure water** - in the morning, dig a pit about 45-50 cm. deep and as wide as a ground sheet or plastic sheet will allow. Toss fresh green branches and waste or impure water into the pit and place a can or cup in the exact centre of the pit. Cover the edge of the plastic with dirt to seal it and place a stone in the centre of the plastic immediately over the position of the can. A groundsheet of clear plastic is always useful for this purpose. This should only give about 1 - 2 litres per day so in desert country, several holes may have to be dug.

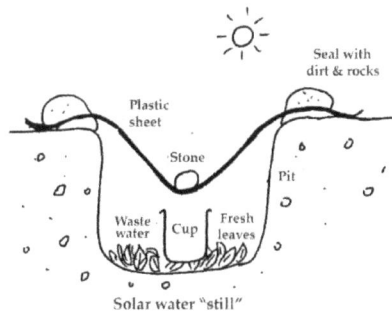

Solar water "still"

- **water condensation from trees** - find a good, safe tree which has plenty of soft, green leaves. Cover a small leafy branch with the largest plastic bag available (or use many) and seal the end with string. Water which transpires from leaves overnight will be collected. Taste with caution as some plants give off toxic vapours.

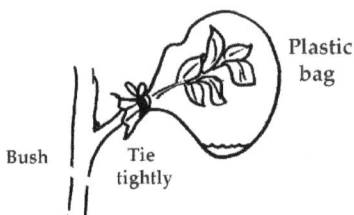

Water from growing plants

3.6 Salt Replacement

With a normal diet, the average person needs about 8-10 grams of salt per day which comes from foods and sometimes a little added salt. The body loses salt in sweat and urine and needs to be replaced regularly.

The amount of salt lost from the body depends upon the temperature and the amount of activity. In hot climate, an extra 4-5 grams may be needed per day for normal activity, but if doing very heavy work, this amount of salt may go as high as 30 grams extra per day.

If the body loses salt faster than it can be replaced then it may experience tiredness, nausea and muscular cramps. This can be remedied by taking a pinch of salt dissolved in about 2 cups (500ml.) of water.

Never take salt as the solid in large amounts.

Whilst walking in hot weather, salt can be replaced in drinks (but do not overdo it - a small pinch/cup) and on foods. Always remember to pack salt in the food supplies as it is very difficult to find salt on inland trips (unless in some salt-lake areas where there is little water anyway!). If near the sea, salt can be obtained from died rock pools or by diluting sea water in emergencies (600 ml. of seawater contains about 15 grams of salt).

Never drink undiluted seawater.

3.7 Water Discipline - one should learn not to waste water. Water use in the bush is different to that at home so it has to be learned and practiced. This does not mean going without water to prove one's "toughness" (= foolishness). Good water practices include:
- reduce sweating not water - keep clothing on to slow perspiration but allow good ventilation;
- drink enough water when thirsty without wasting it;
- use minimal water for washing - use a sponge or absorbent cloth for washing the body;
- use only half a cup of water for cleaning teeth;
- use the water left over from brewing tea etc. for washing up;
- do not drink excessive amounts - swirl the water around the mouth before swallowing; suck lollies if

they are not too sweet;

- do not drink sugary liquids (e.g. soft drink, thick cordials, fruit juices);
- keep dried or salty foods to a minimum;
- do not smoke and drink alcohol excessively;
- keep in the shade as much as possible - keep cool;
- walk in the cool of the day (at night in desert if visibility is good);
- rest as often as possible;
- keep the body (especially the head) wet if there is any spare (even polluted) water;
- do not drink seawater or urine (in emergencies, these can be solar distilled);
- eat good foods remembering that dehydrated food requires considerable water;
- look after hygiene - some problems will cause vomiting and/or diarrhoea, two ways to rapidly lose water; and
- take all opportunities to resupply with water.

Chapter Four: Food

4.1 About Food

The body needs food for energy, replacement and maintenance. There are five main food groups:

- **carbohydrates** - for energy and they include:
  - Sugars - both simple sugars (monosaccharides) e.g. glucose in barley sugar & fructose from fruit, which absorb immediately into the bloodstream and double sugars (disaccharides) e.g. sucrose or table sugar and lactose from milk which all have to be digested (2-3 hours);
  - Starches - as in starchy foods e.g. potatoes, flour in bread and pasta which all need to be digested; and
  - Cellulose - which cannot be digested in Humans but, as fibre, is very important in moving materials through the digestive system.
- **proteins** for replacement and building of new body tissue. It is not destroyed in cooking and is found in meat, fish, milk & cheese, eggs, nuts, beans (e.g. soya beans) and in fruit and vegetables.
- **fats & oils** (fats are solid oils) are richer than sugars for making energy but must be digested over time. They are also sources of some fat-soluble Vitamins (A & D).
- **vitamins** are complex chemicals vital for continued daily health, including:
  - Vitamin A for growth, healthy mucus membranes

and good night vision. In milk, eggs, liver (excess Vitamin A kills if too much liver is eaten), yellow vegetables. Stable when cooked.

- Vitamin B Group for use of sugars in the body, health of nerves, skin & eyes. Not stored for long in the body so must be replaced. Destroyed by cooking and are soluble in water. Meats, cereals, legumes (beans, peas etc.), milk are sources.
- Vitamin C helps resist infection, gives good gums and teeth and binds body cells together (deficiency gives Scurvy). Not stored in the body and is destroyed by drying, heating and dissolves in water.

  Good sources are Citrus Fruits (oranges, lemons etc.), tomatoes, green and red peppers and potatoes.
- Vitamin D helps in the body's use of calcium and phosphorus minerals, vital to bones (deficiency causes Rickets). Made in the skin from sunlight and also found in oily fish (sardines, tuna etc.).
- **Minerals (Salts)** are chemical elements in compounds and are in soluble form which help maintain and regulate the body's functions. These include calcium and phosphorus (for bones, teeth), iodine (for the thyroid gland), potassium and sodium and chloride ions (for the nerves), iron (for red blood cells and oxygen intake). They are found in most foods but some may be lost in excess cooking. with a good diet, mineral and vitamin supplements are not needed. always pack enough table salt (sodium chloride) for

the trip.

4.2 Choice of Foods

Thorough planning about food requirements is necessary before the trip. Factors to be considered are:

- **about the trip**, including the duration of the trip. How many meals are to be needed? Is there a certainty of water on the trip? How heavy will it be?

  A short trip would not require too much economy and more fresh and tinned food can be packed. Longer trips (say, more than three days) will need more concentrated foods which are light in weight. Dehydrated foods are better for long trips but they require more water.

- **type of trip**. Cold or hot weather? Easy walking or tough?

  Usually more energy will be used in tough walking and in colder climates. Cooked meals are going to be preferred more in colder climates and cold, midday meals are better under hot conditions. More water will be needed in hotter weather and fire bans may prevent the use of cooking fires (so rely on cold or pre-cooked foods)

- **size of party**. Can food supplies and cooking be shared? Can everyone cook?

  It may be more useful, in larger groups, for a few to organize the food and cooking but all to share in the burden of carrying the stores. This system breaks down if the party separates splits up.

  For small or medium-sized groups, it still is better if

each person makes their own preparations but share on an informal basis.

- **the nature of the food.** This is often determined by the other factors but should be planned so that it can be easily carried, prepared and is nutritious.

4.3 More on the nature of food

- Energy content requirements are the most important – the body uses about 8000 kJ per day resting (1 kJ or kilojoule is the metric unit of energy = 4.1868 Calories) and a lot more with activity. The amount needed also varies with the body chemistry, gender and age of the person. Some people use more energy than others, woman usually less than men and younger and older people need less than those in the 18-35 age group.

The average, fit person between 18 and 35 years involved in light activity needs about 12 000 kJ per day (MAN) or 8 500 kJ per day (WOMAN). Fats and oils then carbohydrates (sugars, starches etc.) are the best food groups for providing energy. At least sufficient of these must be taken each day. Deficiency causes weakness, faintness and collapse. Sweets, such as Barley Sugar are good as snacks to keep up energy.

- The life of stored foods. Many foods used in our society perish very quickly. Keeping foods cool and in air-tight containers help but some will not last long e.g. frozen meat may last the day, eggs may last a few days (keep wrapped in a rigid container) and some fresh fruit and vegetables will last much longer (oranges, apples, onions, green peppers, potatoes). Nuts last very well as do rice and cereals, tea, flour, dried pastas, sugar, wrapped sweets, biscuits, dried beans, and lentils. All must be kept dry and most should be in sealable plastic bags (double bags if loose powder/grains).

The most useful foods are those which have been dehydrated. These include many vegetables (peas, green beans, potato, mixed vegetables, carrots, onion flakes, mushrooms, tomato slices and celery), some meats (chipped beef, ham), egg, fruits (dates, sultanas, apple, apricot, pineapple, paw-paw, coconut) and many soups, sauces and extras (curry powder, mustard, paprika, spices, pepper and salt, beef and chicken stock cubes for flavouring). Special freeze-dried meals are also available (in packets or cups) but are often expensive and give indigestion if not cooked well. Dried fish and preserved meats (salami, carbonosi, pepperoni etc. - the drier varieties) are very useful.

An excellent meat substitute is T.V.P, (textured vegetable protein made from soya beans) - it makes great meat patties (with onion, stale breadcrumbs and spices with a little cooking oil) and stews (but add beef cubes).

Canned foods are sometimes useful but they are heavy to carry and the cans must be carried out as garbage. Some useful varieties are SMALL cans of meat (ham, corned beef, spam, minced beef), fish (tuna, sardines, salmon), deserts a luxury for short walks, and some meat spreads. Milk is best carried as powdered milk but the condensed milk in a tube is good for tea/coffee. Ultra-High Temperature (U.H.T.) milk will last a while but is bulky to carry. Processed cheese in aluminium foil lasts longer than other forms. Other useful foods come in small sachets. These include jams, honey (good energy source!), vegemite, butter, and sauces.

4.4 Balancing the diet and preparation

For good health, a good mix of all of the main food groups is essential. With a well-planned set of meals, this can be easily achieved. For most walks, the proportion of main groups would most likely be:
70% CARBOHYDRATE
20% PROTEIN and
10% FAT

Preparation should be easy and without fuss. One or two pots should only be necessary. With cookers, such as the Trangia, two cans are often provided. One can is used to cook the single main meal and the other to boil water for tea or coffee, soup and/or noodles with the excess water being used for washing the first can and other items.
Keep food preparation and washing-up to a minimum but be thorough in what is used.

Pre-planning of food is essential for providing enough

food which is easy to carry and prepare. Some people prefer to pre-pack entire meals but usually some flexibility and freedom of choice based on a pre-planned menu is best. Some main meals can be pre-packed as one pot meals.

A good plan for normal weather and country conditions is based on three-meals-a-day plus snacks. It is important to eat and drink when the body needs it, unless in an emergency situation when rationing must be maintained to "stretch" the food and water over the time required for the trip or rescue (at least TWO DAYS SUPPLY of emergency FOOD and WATER should be packed in addition to the normal supplies).

A typical DAILY MENU could be:
BREAKFAST: Cereal (or small, hot meal in cold weather) using rehydrated powdered milk and sugar. Dried fruit as needed. Bread (or toast) with sweet spreads. Tea or Coffee.
LUNCH: (usually eaten cold unless cold weather) Cheese. Dry biscuit (crackers/crisp bread) with meat or fish spreads. Tinned meat or fish or preserved meat. Fruit (fresh or dried). Tea/Coffee or light cordial/water
DINNER: (Main Meal - start after setting-up camp). Rice/pasta (soak well before). Sauce, meats etc. as required. Dried/fresh vegetables. Desert (dried or tinned fruit with custard or instant pudding. Soup/Tea/Coffee (have soup last so that water is boiled only once). Snacks and drinks should be taken whenever needed

throughout the day. These may include: chocolate, dried fruit, fresh fruit (whilst it lasts), muesli or fruit bars, glucose barley sugar (and other sweets), nuts, biscuits or Scroggin (mixture of nuts, dried fruit with possibly sweets and chocolate)

Remember to drink plenty of water with dried foods.

4.5 A Possible Five-Day Plan:
The following chart shows a suggestive five-day menu using appropriate trekking foods. This cycle can be continually repeated if the trek is more than five days.

DAY	ONE	TWO	THREE	FOUR	FIVE
BREAKFAST Winter: substitute oatmeal porridge for cereal. Dried fruit.	Eggs or egg powder, Toast (Ts) Fruit. Tea/coffee(T/C)	Meusli[1] Ts, spread[3] T/C	Cereal[2] Ts spreads T/C	Pancakes (pre-mix in sealed bag). Ts, spreads, T/C	Cereal Ts, spread dried fruits
LUNCH	Bread[4] crackers[5] Cheese, fruit spreads, T/C	Dried meat or fish, bread[4] T/C	Small tin fish, bread, fruit. T/C	Noodles, died meat or fish. T/C	Salami, crackers. Spreads. T/C
DINNER	Main meal. Take time to prepare. Use fresh veg when possible potato, onion, rice. Use SINGLE POT meals (see later). Always best to leave soups until last. Freeze-dried whole meals available. Vary the menu and ensure plenty of water if using dried foods.				
Notes: 1. Muesli bars broken 2. Wheat Bix or All Bran best.3. jams, honey, peanut butter, Nutella in tubes or sachets. vegemite. 4. Tortillas, German black bread, or make damper. 5. incl. crispbreads Powdered or tubed milk, sugar					

4.6 One pot meals.

These are good for the main meal at night and should only require one pot or billy can for cooking. Other pots can be used to boil water for tea/coffee or soup.

Some can be pre-mixed and placed into labelled self-sealed plastic bags and there is a great variety of light-weight, freeze-dried whole meals available in the supermarket or camping store. The best, however, are those made on the spot with as much fresh material as possible. but they are best if mixed on the spot. Some examples include:

- Quick Rice (soak beforehand) partially cooked, then add dried peas, dried ham (or chipped beef, TVP etc.), curry powder or meat sauce flavour;
- Egg Noodles, sliced salami (or dried beef), dried tomato slices, mushroom soup mix.
- Spaghetti (break lengths and partially cook), T.V.P. or dried meat, beef cube, dried onion, spaghetti sauce mix, grated cheese on top when served.
- Quick rice, sweet & sour sauce mix, canned or dried ham, dried pineapple, cashews.
- Quick rice, tinned tuna, cheese or white sauce, dried peas or beans, flaked coconut.
- Quick brown rice, dried beef (or left-over salami etc.), dried mushrooms, dried onions (or fresh is still available), Stroganoff sauce mix,
- Fried rice (boil rice first in min. water then add a little oil), dried ham or bacon (keeps well if dried), onions,

dried peas (boil with rice first).

- Egg powder, dried ham, dried parsley flakes, dried onion (good breakfast in cold weather).
- Fried meat patties made from T.V.P. or dried meat, dried onion, bread crumbs (good use for stale bread/crackers), beef cube, spices (add a little oil and flour to mix it all together). Lightly fry in minimal oil.
- Mixed vegetable noodles, dried mixed vegetables, pepper, vegetable or tomato soup mix.

An example of a pre-planned food pack is the older Army Ration Pack (per man/day) of five separate daily ration packs:

A	B	C	D	E
Ham & Egg	Pork & Beans	Luncheon Meat type II	Sausages & Veg	Beef & Egg
Jam, plum	Jam, raspberry	Jam, apricot	Jam, blackberry	Jam, peach
Curry powder	Curry powder	Curry powder	Soup Pdr, beef	Soup pdr, chicken
Beef & veg	Corn beef	Beef & gravy	Luncheon Meat type I	Corn beef
Dried rice	Dried rice	Dried rice	Potato & onion dried	Potato & onion dried
Peaches	Peaches	Pears	Two fruits	Two fruits

Each pack also contained items common to all including: a cereal block; biscuits (2 packs survival); biscuits (shortbread); cheese (tin); chewing gum; butterscotch lollies; butter (tin); sweetened condensed milk (tube); sugar (12 sachets); teabags (2); instant coffee (2); salt (1 sachet); and fruit drink powder. They also contained a scouring pad, small soap cake, toilet paper (shiny smooth), waterproof matches and a most useful tin opener/spoon.

- Remember to soak rice or pasta well before the meal.
- Use just enough water for the combined dried foods.
- Wash the main pot afterwards.
- Never keep tinned foods once partly used.

4.7 Some Other Recipes.

DAMPER (individual serve) - 250 grams (1 cup) of self-rising flour (add one-quarter teaspoon of baking powder if using plain flour) mixed thoroughly with a small pinch of salt and water to make a stiff dough (mix on flat plate sprinkled with flour). Knead well. Place into a sealed container (e.g. two metals plates held with wire; boiling can with lid or just wrap in alfoil) and cook in coals of an open fire with coals heaped on top. Check often as cooking time will vary.

JOHNNY CAKES - make up a damper dough as before but break it up into small, thin cakes. Cook directly on coals, turning every two minutes.

PUFTALOONS - use a damper mix to make small cakes which are then fried in fat. Sultanas can be added.

SLEDGING BISCUITS – a staple of Antarctic explorers and similar to damper. Make at home using 150g plain white flour, ½ tsp baking soda, ½ tsp salt, 30g butter and

50ml cold water. Melt the butter and rub it into the flour and baking soda mixture. Add water until it is a firm dough and then roll it flat about 1 cm, thick. Prick the surface with holes using a form and then bake in a pre-heated oven at 190C for about 15-20 minutes until golden brown. Cool and wrap in waxed paper.

VEGETARIAN BEEF STEW - cook one half to three-quarters of a cup of rice in enough water then about 60 grams of T.V.P. "beef" chunks, and simmer for about an hour. Add half a packet of vegetable soup, a similar amount (use the packet as a measure) of dried onion, a half packet of dried peas, flour (pre-mixed with hot water) to thicken. Serves two.

PORRIDGE - to half a cup of rolled oats and a cup of water and a handful of dried sultanas and a heaped dessert spoon of sugar. Bring to the boil with constant stirring, simmer for a few minutes and remove it from the flame. Stir in five dessert spoons of powdered milk. There are several varieties of 'Instant oats' available in different flavours in pre-mixed packets – just add water or milk.

PEMICAN – a recipe from the Cree people of North America as a way or preserving meat. Generally, it is an amount of lean meat mixed with about a quarter amount of fat from the same animal, cut finely, thoroughly mixed together and cooked slowly, dried and powdered. Today, 'Beef Jerky' purchased from supermarkets is a good substitute and saves preparation.

HOOSH – a recipe used a lot by Antarctic explorers using about 60 g. per person of dried meat (pemmican or jerky powdered) and add to about 100 g water. Heat and then add about 75 g. of crushed sledging biscuit until the mix is thick. Other things such as dried onion etc. can be added.

4.8 Cooking Hints
- always use low coals if cooking on an open fire;
- stir or turn the food constantly;
- soak dried foods (rice, pasta, dried veges., T.V.P. etc.) well before cooking starts. Rice etc. can be started first;
- use only the amount of water needed - with mixed dried foods, reduce the TOTAL amounts needed for the combined effort (e.g. if one cup of water is needed for rice and another for T.V.P., mix and use one-and-a-half cups);
- always use lids to speed cooking and conserve fuel;
- If using fuel stoves, never re-fill when hot – estimate an excess amount needed for the job and then return excess fuel to the container;
- If in a group, share one cooking fire - several fires are not better than one;
- do not cook inside a tent unless forced to do so by extremes of COLD weather. If so, cook in the opening (but rig a "porch"
  with a groundsheet over a guy rope) on a wide, flat rock with a small stove;
- try to do most of the cooking before dark;
- if using local water (and without purifying tablets), boil a large can full for a good time then allow the excess to stand overnight with a lid on. Pour this into water bottles;

- use the minimum of utensils for cooking and eating – use only one (or possibly two) pots so plan meals beforehand. Thoroughly wash all items immediately after the meal using excess water (made for tea/coffee) in the largest pot;
- compress rubbish (e.g. compact into empty packets) and carry it out to the nearest proper waste dump. The next (desperate) alternative is to compact and deeply bury it (if there is a camp fire - burn waste first) Restore the ground surface to original state.

4.9 Wildfoods

Using local animals, plants and fungi as sources of food should occur only if one's life depends upon it. There are so many varieties of natural things which are poisonous and dangerous that even some of the so-called 'experts' get food poisoning. Only those EXPERIENCED in locating, identifying, trapping or gathering bushfood should attempt to do so. One must be trained by LOCAL indigenous people to really know about the abundance of wildfoods rather than a book. Too many edible plants are similar to poisonous ones, and trapping animals is not easy unless one is skilled.

Hikers should carry at least TWO DAYS emergency food and water, having planned so thoroughly that it is not needed.

PRECAUTIONS - if there is a need to eat wild things then be very cautious. In general:
- avoid anything with red in fruit, leaves or the body in

general;

- never eat decaying matter or animals which look sick;
- cook any meat (lizards, fish, birds etc.) thoroughly to kill any parasites;
- if it smells of bitter almonds or peaches, AVOID;
- avoid plants with a MILKY SAP;
- test a little plant matter on the soft skin of the inside arm. If there is no allergic red reaction or a burning feeling, place a little on the tongue. If there is still no burning sensation, bad taste (giving nausea) or smell, nibble a little, wait and swallow if it does not burn. Wait at least five minutes before eating any more. It is better to taste small portions over a longer time than to eat large amounts at one time.

Those who are able to learn about bush foods from direct learning with an expert should make appropriate notes and add to this book concerning:

PLANTS: local name and description (do a sketch indicating colours) - where found - when in season - part edible - how to collect - how to prepare.

ANIMALS: local name - description(sketch) - where found - signs - how to catch/trap - edible parts - how to prepare.

Remember that most animals and many plants are protected and wildfood should only be used in case of real need.

IN CASE OF EMERGENCY, some very common sources of food which can easily be identified and obtained by the novice are:

FERN FIDDLES - a variety of types (e.g. Mangrove Fern, Swamp Fern, Tree Fern, and Bracken Fern etc.) - ferns are easily identified by their triangular blade of many small leaves jutting out at almost right-angles from a central stalk.

The fiddles are the young leaf which starts as a closed, light-green coil at the base near the trunk - they are common to most of the wetter parts of the country, especially in river valleys and mountains during all seasons:

Fern Fiddles

For softer varieties of ferns, the more recent fiddles can be eaten raw or boiled as a green vegetable.

STINGING NETTLES (*Urtica dioica*) - small, heart-shaped leaves (up to 10 cm. long) with serrated (jagged) edges and the tops of the leaves are covered with many small stinging hairs (CARE!). They have a wide distribution, especially in forests and limestone country.

Do not confuse with the larger stinging tree which is more dangerous. It is usually found in tropical rainforests and is a tree of modest height with large, heart-shaped leaves several centimetres across and covered with large, stinging hairs.

Stinging nettle

Gather only the top leaves of the plant carefully using a piece of cloth or bark over the hand or wear gloves and pull the leaves through the cloth to remove some of the hairs. Make sure that all of the hairs have been removed. Boil thoroughly and eat as a green vegetable or as a base for an herbal tea.

If stung by the nettles, wash with soap and water and cover firmly with some duct tape. Rip off the tape to remove the hairs. Apply a cold compress. Dock weed plant often grows in the same general areas as the stinging nettle plant. The plant grows in height about 60 cm long or more and the leaves are very large, oval and have rounded tips. The lower leaves may have a reddish color to their stems. Crush a few leaves and apply the juice to the nettle rash. Dock leaves can also be boiled and eaten in small amounts.

Dock

CAT'S TAIL (often called "bulrush") - long, slender grey-green leaves with a prominent sausage-shaped brown flowerhead – grows near freshwater streams and lakes in most of the country. Eat the flowerhead raw or cook (boil or on coals) - or shake the flowerheads over or in a cloth and collect the yellow pollen. Mix into a dough with a little water and cook on the coals like a hot-cake.

Cat's Tail or Bull Rushes

PRICKLY PEAR CACTUS Fruits edible as are the thick leaves but pull out spines first and the peel the skin or roast the leaves over the coals for a short time to remove the spikes.

Water from a cactus is generally NOT safe to drink. Some moisture may be obtained as dew off the spines in the morning.

Look for the mauve-red fruit on top. Poke a pointed stick into its top and shave off the outer skin with a knife. Cut off the fruit and eat the outside only, not the seeds inside. Select some of the fresh, top leaves and hold them firmly between two sticks, chop stick style, and cut them off. Holding each down with a stick, scrape off the spikes with the side of a knife. Singe the leaves in a flame to remove any further spines then cook on the coals for about 7-8 minutes or until the surface becomes soft. Scrape off any cinders and cut into strips for eating.

Prickly Pear

BLACKBERRIES – small, black berries of small beads. Care with the spikey stems of the plant when gathering.

Blackberries

GRASSES (many types, including Bamboo) - leaves are long, very thin and rising together from clumps, veins on leaves are parallel - very common - all seeds and the white tips at the base (once pulled out) can be eaten. Grass seeds may be collected, made into a dough with a little water and cooked on the coals. Young Bamboo shoots can be cut off and boiled.

SEAWEEDS - especially the thin, green varieties such as Ulva or 'sea lettuce' and the thin, brown Kombu. Soak in freshwater for a while before cooking as a leaf vegetable or eat raw.

Ulva or Sea Lettuce

PIGFACE – a groundcover plant with succulent (like a cactus) leaves which grows on the coast, especially on dunes. Fruits are good eating and are purple when ripe. The fleshy pulp can be squeezed out and eaten. The leaves are can be eaten if desperate and are very salty.

Pigface

WITCHETTY GRUB (several types - all larvae of moths) - fat, creamy- coloured grubs found in tree-trunks where they bore out the wood

Look for "sawdust" at the base of trunks and limbs –
especially in sickly trees, especially wattles. Find a bulge
in the trunk not far from the base and cut into the tree to
find the grub.

Witchetty Grub

First remove the entrails by holding the head between the
left fingers and squeezing the end of the body along to
the anus. Eat all but the head of the grub. Eat raw or cook
on the coals.

LIZARDS, FISH, BIRDS and SNAKES (most - if you can
catch them and they don't get you first!) - cut off the head
and gut it. Cook in the skin on hot coals. Use a long,
sharpened stick with three prongs at its end with cut
barbs. Wrap a stone in between the barbs to give it
weight.

OYSTERS and other molluscs on the seashore. Take care
with some molluscs, especially those brightly coloured,
and test the flesh cautiously.

Taste "wildfoods" with much caution.

Chapter Five: Fire

5.1 In General
Fire can be both a friend or foe depending upon how, where and when it is used.

Open fires should never be used when there is a local fire ban or in parks or places where they are not allowed. If open fires are permitted and conditions are suitable (**never** in strong, hot winds in dry, vegetated country), then they must only be lit in **well-made fire pits** which will limit their spread (see later).

Fires must be kept as small as possible depending upon the need and size of the party. One fire for the party is better than many individual fires. Before making the firepit of ring of rocks, the immediate area should be cleared of all leaves and grass and any over-hanging branches removed. These preparations and the gathering of suitable dry, dead firewood should be done well before dark. Enough firewood must be gathered to last the night and into the next morning.

5.2 Types of Fires
Fires may include:

COOKING FIRES - are usually small and the best meals are made on or in the coals and ashes at the edges of the fire with cooking pots placed in the centre of secure coals or hung on supports (see later).

Some foods could also be cooked directly in the ashes (e.g. potatoes wrapped in foil) or on a flat, fine-grained rock on or at the edge of the fire (e.g. meat strips, eggs).

CAMP FIRES - for light and warmth need not be big but may be bigger than the cooking fire (probably made by adding more wood to the cooking fire). Like all fires, it should be in a fire pit and/or surrounded by stones.

SLEEPING FIRES - not recommended unless in extreme cold and may be longer and narrower but must also be in well-cleared pits so that fire does not spread to the sleepers. These fires are best tended throughout the night on a rostered duty system if conditions are extreme.

Alternatively, one can use the stones around the edge of the fire to heat the inside of the tent by either wrapping them in sacking material carried for this purpose (as a pack liner) or by placing stones in an empty boiling tin which the lid placed on top. These stone heaters do not last for long and care must be taken when taking the stones from the fire,

A good way to carry emergency water in the pack is to use a large hot water bottle. The water bottle can then be filled with hot water before retiring and the bottle placed in the sleeping bag at the feet or behind the back.

Care should always be taken with fires:

- never throw kerosene (paraffin), alcohol or empty gas containers (or any other pressurized container) into the fire;
- clearly label fuel containers, which should be metal, so that they are not mistaken for water bottles;
- before retiring for the night ensure that the fire is well-contained or extinguished completely;
- before leaving the site, completely extinguish the fire, dig-in the ash and recover the pit with the original sod which was dug out.

5.3 Making Fire

A fire can be started with dry fuel in plenty of air by the use of:

WAXED MATCHES - a good, general fire-maker. Carry in water-proofed container such as an old pill bottle with a length of "striker" inside. Waxed matches can be made by dripping wax from a lighted candle over a match - rub off the wax from the head prior to striking.

When striking a match, "stab" it at the leading end of the striker strip rather than drawing it across.

If matches are WET, then dry them by rolling them in the hair (non-oily) or in dry toilet paper.

CIGARETTE LIGHTER – metal army type with flip-top lid is the best but ensure that it is full of fuel and paste spare flint in the lid.

Even if there is no fuel, the flint is useful for putting a

spark into tinder (e.g. dry wood shavings, clothing fluff, fine dead grass, pine needles, shredded inside of tree bark, dead fungi, rotted wood dust etc. In damp weather, keep some spare tinder and small twigs in a dry place in the top of the pack.

MAGNIFYING LENS - useful only in strong sunlight but works well with fine tinder. The lens may come from the First Aid kit, camera or binoculars. Some spectacles may also be strong enough.

FLINT & STEEL - commercial versions with a cylindrical flint and a saw blade are available but any old lighter flint can be sparked along a serrated knife or old hacksaw blade carried for that purpose. Always a good back-up, especially in wet weather.

WOOD BOW - works well only with much practice, patience and very dry tinder. It can be made by:

1. make a small (60-80 cm.) bow from a pliable sapling and string, vine or bootlace;
2. cut a hardwood spindle - about 20-30 cm. long with circular diameter about 1 cm. and round both ends;
3. use a knife to gouge a small hollow at the end of a piece of softwood and cut a hole below it (i.e. on the other side) to take the spindle and a little tinder;
4. wind the bowstring once around the spindle,

position the hand-support (a mug or small block with an indentation gouged out in the middle) on the top of the spindle;

5. place the other tip of the spindle into the small hole in the softwood base;

6. move the bow back-and-forth whilst pressing firmly on the hand-support
    to obtain a small ember in the carved
    notch & tinder;

7. when a slight glowing ember has been produced, blow on it carefully to keep it alight and add a little more tinder until a flame is produced; the

8. carefully transfer the burning embers into a previously-stacked pile of light, dry timber)

This can also be done with practice using the hands clasped together to rotate the spindle without the need for a bow, but it requires a good knowledge of wood and hard work.

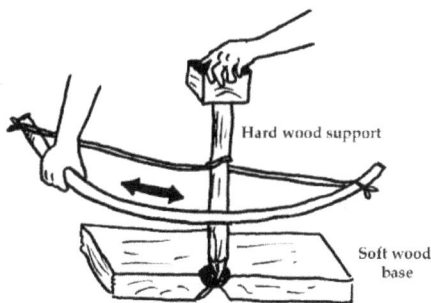

A Wood Bow

5.4 Fires & Fireplaces

Build minimal-sized fireplaces appropriate to the conditions. A good fireplace prevents the spread of fire, protects it from the wind and provides a good cooking area.

Clear an area about 2 metres across in a sheltered position away from trees and over-hanging branches remove leaves and roll up the turf (or remove grass). The fireplace can now be built in the middle of this area. Fireplaces include:

BASIC STONE CIRCLE - make a circle of dry, hard, non-porous stones (porous stones which give a hollow sound when hit may contain water which will cause the stone to explode upon heating) with larger ones on the windward side and flat, smooth stones at front for direct cooking.

Simple stone circle

YUKON STOVE - a more elaborate stone fireplace suitable for more permanent camp in very cold conditions. They are made when there is plenty of stones and time:

1. clear an open area of earth and dig a circular hole about 20-30 cm. deep and about 30-40 cm across, but the diameter depends upon amount of rock and effort available
2. Dig a steep-sided channel at one side leading steeply into the hole for air ventilation;
3. collect large, dense stones (not porous nor layered types) and, using wet mud/clay and the rocks, build a tall, circular chimney around the hole;
4. Place tinder, kindling and wood into the pit and light from the channel with a long stick.

This gives a very warm, safe fireplace which also allows cooking on top.

A Yukon fireplace

TRENCH FIRE - provides good shelter from wind and is a good general-purpose fire for warmth and cooking. To make this:

1. Clear an area is cleared and roll the turf back;
2. dig a trench about 90 cm. long (longer with a big party), 30 cm. wide and about 30 cm. deep;
3. the fire is then built in the pit.

For mass cooking, a layer of large stones can be placed in first and a good fire built on top. Volcanic stones are preferred as they must be solid, and non-porous. When the fire has died away, the ashes can be swept to the side or completely removed with green branches to expose the hot stones for cooking.

Native peoples, such as the New Zealand Māori have used a traditional hāngi for centuries by wrapping foods in broad leaves (with no stinging hairs nor milky sap) such as banana or cabbage leaves or even aluminium foil. Sprinkle the stones with a little water to make some steam and place the bundles on the stones. These may then be covered with a layer more leaves or an old sack which has been soaked in water. Cover carefully with dirt from the edges inwards ensuring that none of it reaches the food bundles, leave it for a number of hours depending upon the amount and type of food, say about 3 hours. Some practice and experience are needed here.

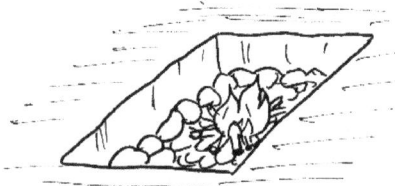

A trench fireplace

RAFT FIREPLACE - useful when the ground is swampy or damp and unable to be cleared. To make this:
1. construct a simple raft about 40-50 cm square using strong, green sticks bound with grass, reeds or twine;
2. place the raft on the most solid ground or raise slightly with stones or more sticks;
3. cover the centre with dirt or mud;
4. build the small fire in the middle.

In snowy forests, the raft can be raised well above the snow using uprights at the corners with two being longer to act as supports. The fires are often called Temple Fires. In true snowy alpine conditions, one should always try to retreat to below the snowline and seek shelter within trees or low bushes but this is not possible then rock shelters are the next best refuge. In extreme conditions a snow cave may have to be dug. In both of these events, alcohol or gas-fueled stoves are necessary.

A temple fireplace

A wind break made similarly to the raft may be stood vertically on the windward side.

TEEPEE FIRE – is the most common type of fire and can be used in any of the previously describe fireplaces. They are best when there is minimum kindling and lighting a fire is difficult. To make this fire:

1. choose a good location against the wind such as a sheltered bank or even a large hollow tree or between buttress roots of large trees. A windbreak may have to be constructed from sticks, rocks or dirt;
2. make a small bed of open kindling such as small twigs, dried leaves, dry bark, whittled shavings of logs etc. Under wet conditions, take the kindling from above ground e.g. peel bark from trees and take the inside part or carefully take timber scraps from inside of large hollow logs (care! spiders & snakes);

3. build up a triangular "teepee" around it. Do not over-load the pile;
4. light the base of the kindling from several sides. If wet, use a small piece of rubber tire (always useful to have in the pack) or a lump of solid fuel (never throw liquid fuels onto a fire!);
5. add more sticks around the sides so as to not topple the structure. Gradually add bigger sticks and logs in a vertical manner.

SQUARE FORT FIRE - is another way of constructing a good fire which will allow air to circulate and is useful is some timber is damp. It can also be used with any fireplace. To make this fire:

1. around a small, open stack of kindling, construct a square "fort" of sticks, each layer resting on the two parallel sticks below;
2. after several layers (to a height of about 15-20 cm.), lay a "roof" of open, light sticks across the top;
3. place another layer of sticks on this at 90 degrees. Several layers of bigger sticks may follow, especially if they are damp.

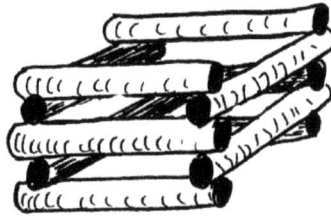

A hollow fort fire

5.5 Fireplace Accessories

Some useful additions to the basic fireplace may help comfort and cooking. These include:

HEAT REFLECTOR - make a small raft of green logs by lashing them together (over-and-under) and angle the raft on its long edge to reflect heat. Metal or aluminium foil can be used to line this windbreak. Do not use Space Blankets as they often have a plastic component.

COOKING SUPPORTS - such as a cross-beam, a triangle or an angled rod can be made from strong, green forked saplings lashed together (use a wire hook for hanging or cut a stick with a convenient fork):

Cooking supports

A multiple hook for
hanging cooking pots

A dingle stick is a more elaborate swinging rod support ideal for holding pots of stew which needs constant checking. To make a dingle stick:

1. drive a forked upright into the ground at the side of the fire;
2. support a long, green rod over the top of the fork so that the rod is supported about mid-way or a little less (ensure that there is a fork for hanging the pot at its smaller end);
3. Tie the other end to the upright by cord or a vine. This should allow the rod to be swung sideways.

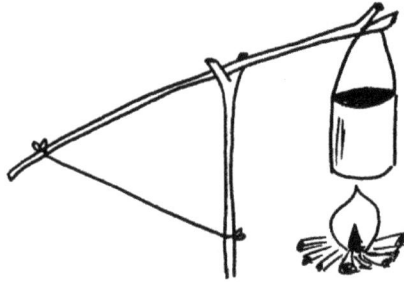

A dingle stick

5.6 Putting Out the Fire

All fires must be extinguished completely so that even the ash is not still smoldering immediately after use, especially if there is a strong wind blowing.

Before leaving the campsite:
- completely extinguish the fire move bigger logs apart;
- cover completely with sand (water first if plentiful); and
- restore the area to its original position if not returning to the site.

Don't be the cause of a wildfire

5.7 Trapped in a Wildfire

Wildfires are a natural part of the country, especially during long, hot, dry summers.

Do not plan trips if there is an extreme fire warning.

In fires, most people die because of **heat exhaustion** due to the radiant heat of the fire because the body ceases to function when there is too much heat. This can even occur if the flames are well away from the body.

Death can also be caused by excessive burns, **searing of the lungs** by super-heated air or other gases, **anoxia** (being overcome by smoke due to lack of oxygen); and by **poisoning** by gases such as carbon monoxide.

Smoke, flames and the general spectacle of the bushfire will panic many people into irrational acts which will also lead them into death by heat exhaustion.

SAFETY PRECAUTIONS - radiant heat (the main killer) travels in straight lines, so the best protection is to get behind a protective barrier e.g. thick tree trunk, earth mound or bank, stones, vehicles, and buildings.

Even clothing will stop a certain amount of radiant heat, so wear loose non-flammable clothing (non-synthetic) which covers most of the body including the head. Cover the body with water if possible and **leave the area immediately**. If caught in the field:

- don't panic
- select an area of with minimal vegetation (not on hillsides where fires move up)

- Seek shelter behind or under protection (e.g. rocks, in a trench, buildings, in or under vehicles - there is little fear of petrol explosion). If in open country, dig a small trench and cover the body with earth with a wet item of clothing over the face. Shelter in natural waterways (at ground level) but never in water tanks or swimming pools.
- keep calm and wait until the flame front passes.

Chapter Six: Weather

6.1 In General

The weather patterns of a local area are influenced by:

- general climate - in turn, due to latitude and;
- distance from the sea - the sea does not vary in its temperature as much as the land so it helps to cool coastal lands in summer and warm them in winter. A similar effect also occurs between day and night. Inland regions tend to have more extreme conditions;
- vertical height - air temperature becomes colder with increase in height (approx. 7^0C degrees every 1000 metres) and
- physical relief (shape and height) of the local country such as:
    - mountain barriers preventing prevailing winds travelling inland and helping to push moist air up the windward sides giving rain but little rain on the lee side as a rain shadow;
    - bare cliff faces causing powerful updrafts due to the heating of air (hot air rises) near the hot rock face;
    - narrow valleys which may funnel strong winds into narrow gorges;
    - broad, open plains which allow for full exposure of prevailing winds.

It is a wise precaution to know about some of the local variations in the overall climatic patterns. Walkers are often trapped in sudden local changes in the weather which are well-known to locals. For example, the weather conditions in mountainous areas can suddenly change with a shift in the wind. What was once a hot trek in mid-summer can suddenly become an alpine sleet squall or even snow with freezing conditions. Trekking down river canyons and in river caves can also be treacherous with sudden rainstorms higher up in the headwaters of the river causing flash flooding downstream. Try not to attempt major trips in known times and areas of climatic difficulties and always take wet/cold weather clothing and extra food and water in case of sudden weather changes.

When looking at weather forecasts, remember that low pressure and high humidity (especially with winds blowing in off the sea) often mean bad weather.

6.2 Reading the Clouds
Clouds are formed from the condensation of water vapour droplets during atmospheric change.
They are the most reliable indicator of local weather changes. Sometimes they can be used to predict a change in the local weather pattern over the next few days as well as heralding an approaching storm.

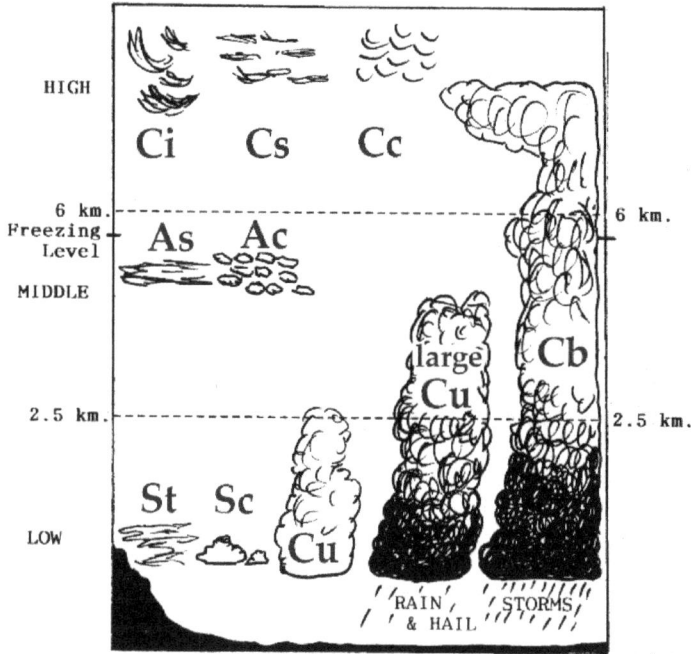

Major cloud types

The main types of clouds are:

LOW CLOUDS
(St) Stratus - thin, extensive, forms fog when touches the ground. Damp as fog but usually no rain (perhaps a little drizzle but it soon clears);

(Sc) Stratocumulus - extensive layer of lumpy white (sometimes light grey) folds. Usually fine weather but occasional showers if they become thicker (and grey coloured). Soon clears;

(Cu) Cumulus - white, fluffy clouds as isolated lumps. Fine weather but if they join and thicken (becoming grey and taller) they could give rain;

(Cb) Cumulonimbus - form during hot, humid days, developing as very tall, thick grey clouds which flatten into an anvil shape at top. Rain and hail with strong storm winds and lightning. Hail if a yellow-green tinge lower down and snow if this is a greener colour. Once these start to develop, <u>seek shelter</u>.

(Ns) Nimbostratus (not shown) - extensive, lead grey sheet covering most of the sky uniformly with oppressive humidity. Lengthy period of rain.

MEDIUM LEVEL

(As) Altostratus - an extensive light greyish veil through which the disk of the sun or moon can only just be seen. As these disks disappear the cloud thickens and becomes greyer, the cloud may give drizzle;

(Ac) Altocumulus - flat sheet of separated small fluffy clouds. Usually after storms and means fine weather.

HIGH LEVEL

These clouds usually are composed of ice crystals due to the higher cold air. They may indicate a possible change in the weather in the next few days:

(Ci) Cirrus or Altocirrus (Mare's Tails) white, thin wisps or streaks. Usually form during fine weather but a change may come within two days if they are getting bigger and the sky beyond is darkening;

(Cs) Cirrostratus - more extensive, fine white wisps which often produce a halo around the sun or moon due to the refraction of light by the ice crystals. Generally, if the halo gets smaller, rain may be coming; larger and it may be fine;

(Cc) Cirrocumulus - (a mackerel sky - looks like the scales on a mackerel fish) high, parallel broken bands of small fluffy cloud. Usually after a storm, clearing to a blue sky.

REMEMBER: The sky is to be watched for changes in the cloud which may indicate a change in the weather in the near future. DO NOT WAIT for the change to happen. If it looks like it is going to be bad - seek shelter well before the event and wait until it clears.

6.3 Other Indicators

Many examples of Weather Lore may have some basis in fact. Early societies were very observant and animals are more aware of changes in pressure and temperature than Humans. Some other natural indicators are:

- Red sky in the morning, sailors take warning, – applies more to the Northern Hemisphere climates, but as much of our weather patterns come from the WEST, a red western sky (filled with water droplets and possibly cirrus cloud to reflect the morning sun from the east) may suggest a change for the worst;
- Animal migration - look for flights of birds or larger animals (e.g. cattle) moving rapidly together in one direction, seeking shelter from an approaching storm (coming from the opposite direction). SEEK SHELTER;
- Ants - building ground nest entrances higher or an

excited throng heading up trees etc. Expect rain soon;

- Sudden change in wind direction - as a pressure cell (especially a LOW or CYCLONE) is approaching, the winds will swing around to the left (e.g. winds coming from the East or Easterlies will swing around and become Northerlies). There also may be a slight drop in the wind speed. Before the storm hits there will probably be considerable disturbance in the wind with a sudden increase in speed with a variety of directions;
- Early morning mist - usually lifts later in the morning to give a fine day. If it thickens then it will not soon lift but become rain-bearing;
- Clear early evening skies - will probably stay clear and stable but there will be colder temperatures early in the morning with frost in the cooler months;
- Rainbow in the afternoon - means that the weather will now become fine.

6.4 Winds

It is useful to know about the usual air mass and wind directions of the national and local area. Whilst these vary greatly and are affected by local terrain, they can give a broad picture of potential weather conditions.

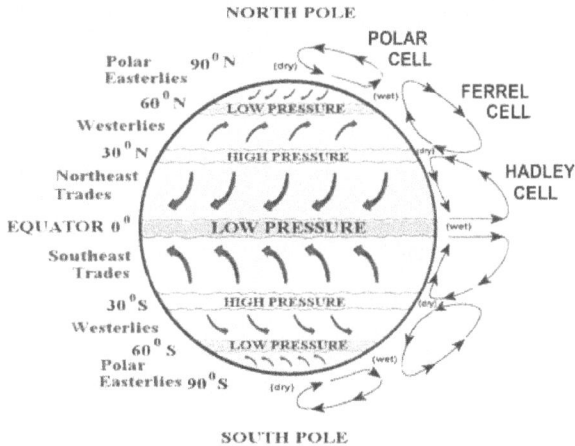

In general terms, winds travel from zones of high air pressure to zones of low pressure. The average air pressure at sea level is:

101.325 kilopascals(kPa)

1,013.25 hectopascals (hPa), 1,013.25 millibars (mbar),

760 mm of mercury,

29.9212 inches of mercury, or

14.696 pounds per square inch (psi).

Air pressure is measured by barometers and some electronic devices and watches have capabilities for measuring air pressure.

Certain regions have prevailing winds as shown on the world map above e.g. eastern **Australia** has south east trade winds which sometimes veer around to the south and bring sudden cold wet, southerly busters. These can also affect the Southern Highlands and Tasmania and bring sudden sleet or snow, even in summer. Western and southern Australia are subject to westerly winds which can bring cold fronts across the continent from west to east. Northern Australia, especially the northeast coast, is subject to hot monsoonal conditions of humid heat and rain and these areas are also subject to Tropical Cyclones (hurricane/typhoons) in summer. In the interior, lack of wind and intense heat during the day and cold nights can be hazardous.

In mid-latitudes of North America, Europe and Asia, winds generally move west to east as Westerlies. In the United States, the weather patterns also follow winds in a west to east movement. In late summer to early fall in North America, a monsoon change often occurs bringing moist air over the Pacific Ocean and Gulf of Mexico which travels north and west to the dry areas of the western United States. The southern and eastern parts of North America are also subject to a summer hurricane season about this time.

In cyclone (hurricane, typhoon) seasons in the late summer of tropical countries, a cyclone warning signal is usually given on the local radio stations, so it is useful to have a small pocket radio if within range of stations and near the coast. If this is heard, the trip should be stopped and all should return to the nearest safe location.

If in the field when a Tropical Cyclone is due to strike:
- start preparing as soon as you can if you cannot make it back to a solidly-built dwelling;
- look for natural protection against:

- high winds
- flying objects
- falling trees
- torrential rain and
- local flooding
- avoid coastlines, rivers, flat open areas;
- seek rock shelters, large rocks or large fallen trees;
- make a small hollow at the base of isolated rocks or fallen trees and try to prepare for wind and rain;
- do not hide in standing hollow trees as rainforest trees have shallow roots and are easily blown over;
- if caught in the open, seek a natural hollow in the lowest point of ground (but NOT creek beds which will flood).

Remember: as the tropical cyclone passes, it will become calm as the eye passes overhead. if you cannot make shelter in that time, stay where you are.

FORCE	DESCRIPTION	VELOCITY (km./hr.)	EFFECTS SEEN
0	CALM	less than 2	smoke rises vertically
1	LIGHT AIR	2-5	direction shown by smoke only
2	LIGHT BREEZE	6-10	wind felt on face;leaves flutter
3	GENTLE BREEZE	11-16	leaves in constant motion
4	MODERATE BREEZE	18-26	small branches move;dust raised
5	FRESH BREEZE	27-34	small trees begin to sway
6	STRONG BREEZE	35-43	large branches in motion
7	NEAR GALE	45-53	whole trees move;difficult to walk
8	GALE	54-64	twigs broken off trees
9	STRONG GALE	66-75	large limbs broken off
10	STORM	77-88	trees uprooted
11	VIOLENT STORM	90-101	widespread damage
12	HURRICANE	102 +	countryside is devastated

The Beaufort Scale of wind speed

Wind chill factor is a major consideration in walking in areas where winds may be prevalent and the climate is wet. - even a gentle breeze will lower temperature by evaporation. In cold, windy conditions, especially if the body is wet, a person can die of hypothermia (exposure) in a few minutes.

Wind chill factor

SPEED (km./hr.)							TEMPERATURE (°C)						
Calm 5	2	-1	-4	-7	-9	-12	-15	-18	-20	-23	-26	-29	
8	1	-1	-4	-7	-9	-12	-15	-18	-20	-23	-26	-29	-32
16	-1	-7	-9	-12	-15	-18	-23	-26	-29	-32	-37	-40	-43
24	-4	-9	-12	-18	-20	-23	-29	-32	-34	-40	-43	-45	-51
32	-6	-12	-15	-18	-23	-26	-32	-34	-37	-43	-45	-51	-54
40	-9	-12	-18	-20	-26	-29	-34	-37	-43	-45	-51	-54	-59
48	-12	-15	-18	-23	-29	-32	-34	-40	-45	-48	-54	-57	-62
56	-12	-15	-20	-23	-29	-34	-37	-40	-45	-51	-54	-59	-62
64	-12	-18	-20	-26	-29	-34	-37	-43	-48	-51	-57	-59	-65

No Extra Effect above 64°C	LITTLE DANGER	INCREASING DANGER - FLESH MAY FREEZE IN 1 MINUTE	GREAT DANGER - FREEZING IN 30 SEC.

Hypothermia occurs when the body loses heat faster than it can produce heat, causing a dangerously low body temperature. Normal body temperature is around 37 C (98.6 F) and hypothermia may occur as if the body temperature falls below this temperature. Left untreated, hypothermia can lead to complete failure of the heart and respiratory system and eventually to death. It is more dangerous for children and older people.

Someone with hypothermia usually isn't aware of their condition because its onset is gradual and the person may also become confused and this can lead to risk-taking behaviour.

Symptoms include:
- Slurred speech or mumbling
- Slow, shallow breathing
- Weak pulse
- Clumsiness or lack of coordination
- Drowsiness or very low energy
- Confusion or memory loss
- Loss of consciousness
- Bright red, cold skin (in infants)

To warm the body back to a normal temperature, one should provide all round gentle warmth (NOT sudden heat). This can be done by:
- removing the person from the source of the chill – out of the wind and remove wet clothing;
- provide warm clothing or place them in a dry sleeping bag;
- keep them horizontal or sit the person down and huddle with them if this is not possible;
- give warm drinks (NOT alcohol).

If extreme with little response to the above methods seek urgent medical assistance!

Chapter Seven: Shelter

7.1 In General
Shelter is a major concern when staying in the field overnight. Without adequate shelter the body is subject to:
- rapid heat loss or gain;
- exposure to the Sun's ultra violet rays;
- exposure to wind, rain or snow; and
- to insect and other pests.

Even under the best conditions of mild weather, the body needs to be protected. For general field work, the shelter should be:
- waterproof;
- strong;
- well-ventilated
- lightweight; and
- able to reduce sunlight.

7.2 types of shelter
Some of types of field shelters include:

A-FRAME OR DOME TENTS - are the best general-purpose shelter, especially if they have a built-in insect screen and a matching fly (cover) which is erected overhead for added protection. The best material is a lightweight fabric such as a synthetic or cotton (japara) which should be water-proof. Synthetic tents are adequate but tend to have inadequate water-proofing and encourage internal condensation. They are however, stronger and lighter than canvas or cotton.

Small A-frame tents, whilst suitable for short duration trips requiring light-weight equipment, are cramped, do not give any headroom, are subject to internal condensation and icing and are hot in summer. Comfortable use depends upon an intelligent selection of the site and the use of a fly. Many problems are overcome if the tent has closeable ventilation windows.

MARQUEE TENTS - are usually of good, waterproofed canvas and give good headroom and storage space. They are better for base camps where equipment does not have to be carried in. They are also heavy, difficult to erect and tend to collect water and snow on the roof.

LEAN - TO's – with one large strip of good waterproof material stretched across a single horizontal rope between two trees. These can be simply erected in a hurry, are well-ventilated and are lightweight. They are very good for hot, tropical conditions but do not give much protection against the wind unless sited properly, preferably near a natural windbreak. A good ground-sheet and insect net (or hammock with net) must also be used.

A good example of these shelters is the army's 'tents-half shelter' or 'hutchie', especially the variety which had a hood in its centre and can also be used as a poncho over person and pack. Ensure that it has side clips so that two can be clipped together to make a decent, sized A-frame tent.

Even a single Half Shelter can be erected between two trees as an A-frame over a hammock and mosquito net swinging below.

BUSH SHELTERS – can be made in an emergency if one is caught out without a tent. They take time and appropriate bush material to build so the site and time must be chosen well in advance of nightfall,

7.3 Choosing a Good Site

Whenever possible, the campsite should be chosen and prepared well before sunset (at least 2 hours). The site should be:

- safe and on high ground;
- protected from wind;
- slightly flat to allow drainage; and
- near fuel & water.

Take care NOT to erect a tent:

- too close to a lake shore or a river bank which could rise with flooding or be a watering hole or entry for animals;
- under dead trees nor those known to lose limbs (e.g. some white gums);
- on tracks and animal trails;
- near the edge of a cliff;
- in gullies or dry water courses which could become flooded;

- on wind-swept ridges; nor
- near insect and other animal nests and holes.

7.4 Erecting the Shelter

After choosing the site which best makes use of the ground and natural protection:

- level-off the ground as carefully as possible as unlevel ground puts an uneven strain on ropes;
- clear the ground of stones, sticks, weeds and roots; and
- sweep away leaves which may contain insects and spiders.

A-FRAME TENTS:

1. Unroll and lay out flat on the site so that the main entrance is downhill and not facing the prevailing wind (check the wind direction or look at the permanent bend in small trees);
2. Strongly peg the corners, sides and doors using appropriately strong (stainless steel is best) hooked pegs. Wider and longer pegs are needed for sand and snow and then supplemented with rocks or logs. Pitons for bare rock where cracks are available;
3. Firmly push end poles into the ground (at least 30 cm. if ground is soft) or make a firm base with pegs or stones. Strongly guy-rope poles. An alternative is to make use of small saplings instead of end poles;
4. Raise the horizontal rope and attach to end poles. Some tents have spikes on the top of the poles which fit through eyelets on the ends of the roof.

Alternatively, a strong but light horizontal ridge pole may be used (depending upon the type of tent). This may be supported on Y-shaped end poles (cut from saplings) and tied or wired into place. The rope or the ridge pole may pass through the tent or the tent may be slung underneath.

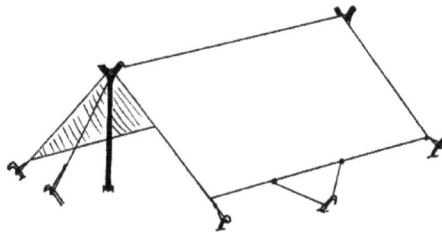

A simple A-frame tent

Carefully-positioned tent
(seen from above)

5. With the ridge pole or rope strongly fixed, the corner guy ropes and then the side ropes are pulled out until the roof of the tent is both stretched tight and rectangular without any creases (which are produced by uneven tension on the guy-ropes). All guy-ropes must be securely fixed to strong stakes using non-slip knots or clips. The bottom edge of the roof should be no less than 15 cm. from the ground and may be kept straight by attaching a small pole horizontally along its length;
Doors and windows should be laced-up and

readjustments made to the guy-ropes to equalize tension over the tent's surface so that there are no sagging parts;

6. Dig a small trench (10-15 cm. deep and 15 cm. wide) around the back and sides of the tent, allowing a good run-off channel downhill. Pile the dirt on the INSIDE of the trench as an extra dam but keep it away from the wall of the tent (use a log if necessary);

7. Erect a FLY TENT over the main tent for extra protection from driving rain, snow or strong sun.

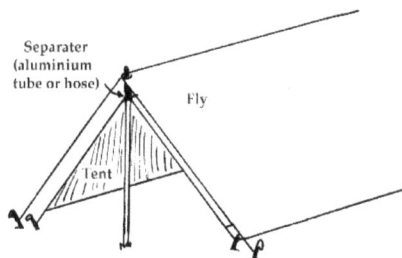

Erecting the fly tent

A good variation of the A-frame arrangement for lightweight hiking is the use of two army tents half shelter and a hammock made from parachute netting. The hammock is erected first between two saplings and then the tents (clipped together) are erected over it so that they are well above ground. This is excellent in warmer climates as there is a free circulation of air. No heavy bedding is needed, only a sleeping bag. A mosquito net can be slung over the horizontal rope before the tent is placed over it.

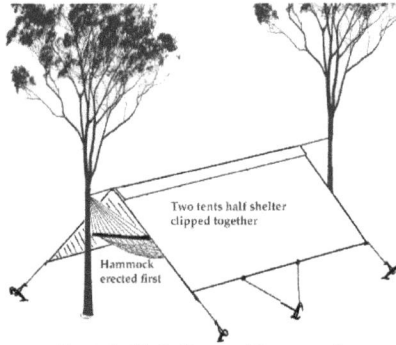

Tents half shelter and hammock

MARQUEE TENTS:

These are more suitable for a large, static base camp with the tent and its equipment being carried in by car or 4WD. The best way of erecting a marquee tent is to:

1. Unroll the tent and lay it flat and square with the roof uppermost;
2. Hammer in guy-ropes (two per corner) 1.5 to 2.0 metres out in both directions from each corner:

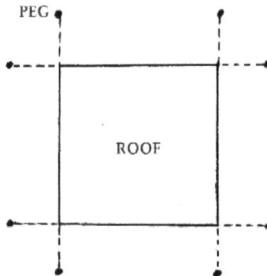

3. Erect corner poles inside (if rough-cut, they should not be green) and guy to pegs with separate ropes;
4. Erect centre pole(s) and ensure a good pitch of the roof on all sides of the centre (rain will collect here if not fully stretched);
5. Peg down walls with foot ropes at corner pegs (or use other pegs to hold down the base of each wall);
6. Lace-up doors and walls;
7. Erect any awnings using separate poles and pegs;
8. Dig a trench around all four sides with a drain running downhill.

LEAN-TO SHELTER:
Ideal for light-weight hiking for an overnight stay. Army tents half-shelter are designed for such a structure:
1. Select a flat, sheltered spot (with the wind across the front of or behind the shelter depending upon the type of weather) making use of natural cover or ground for protection (not under a tree or branch likely to fall);
2. Erect forked poles about 2 metres apart - guy if necessary or use existing small saplings;
3. Stretch a firm rope between the poles or use a ridge pole. Lash the ends to the uprights (use a square lashing using twine or vines). Alternatively, one can use two telescopic poles which have spikes for slotting into the gromets of the tent. If so, the poles will need to be supported in two directions;
4. Stretch the roof material (plastic or canvas) down from the ridge pole to the ground at an angle of about 45 degrees (steeper if snow or heavy rain is likely) and

strongly peg the base (use large, flat rocks or a heavy log as an alternative). Side poles from the top of the uprights to the ground at the roof will give extra support. These should be lashed at the uprights as well as at the ground:

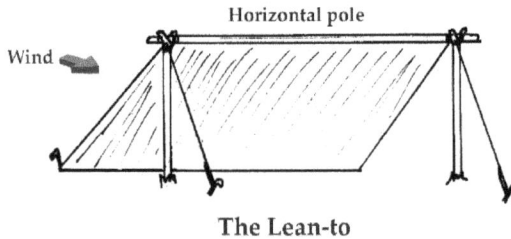

The Lean-to

If one is not carrying a tent and has to construct a basic one from what is being carried or from natural coverings (only in an emergency), then:

1. make up a light rectangular frame about 2 metres x 1.5 metres from dead saplings strongly lashed at the corners;

2. Support by uprights (as before) so that the frame is angled at 45 degrees and lash extra poles (about 30 cm. apart) onto the frame parallel to the long side;

3. Weave thin, green saplings through these at right-angles (i.e. down the roof); and

4. then cover with plastic sheet or broad green leaves, bark or ferns so that they start from the top edge of the roof and overlap down to the ground. Some extra weaving will be needed in heavy winds:

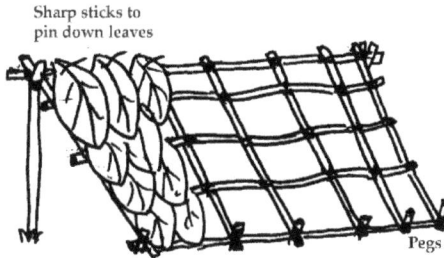

Sharp sticks to
pin down leaves

Pegs

The Bush Lean-to

For maximum comfort, lean-tos should be kept low to the ground and small. If built so that the front is across the wind, then a small fire could be built in front allowing one to sleep with the feet towards the fire (the cross-wind ensures that no embers go into the lean-to).

The ground beneath the lean-to must be covered with another sheet of plastic or with dry leaves, grass or ferns. never sleep on the bare ground as too much body heat will be lost.

(CARE! - do not use poisonous plants with red colours or milky sap of some broad-leave plants and take care of Stinging Trees which have fine hairs on their broad leaves).

7.5 Other Improvised Shelters

It takes considerable time to erect shelter even under good conditions. Whilst walking, one should keep a constant lookout for possible natural shelters in case of a sudden change in the weather. These may be:

- rock overhangs (on the lee or protected side);

- caves;
- hollow trees;
- large fallen trees;
- low, dense thickets;
- hollows in the ground; or
- steep mounds or dunes.

Take care as these places may be the home of animals such as snakes, spiders or larger animals so they should be checked carefully before being entered and then swept with grass or bracken.

Using improvised shelters depend upon the surroundings as both a part of the protection plan and as a source of raw materials.

The type of climate also determines the type and degree of protection of the shelter:

RAINFOREST - protection from rain and cold in the winter months in some area. Hollow trees are good for a short stay but otherwise a lean-to (as described) may be necessary

An alternative to the Lean-to, is the pigmy hut. This is made from a hemispherical frame of light, flexible (green) saplings which have been bent over to form a half circle and the ends firmly planted into the ground around in a circle. Holes may have to be made first by hammering a sharp stick into the ground using a large rock.

The top of the roof (where the half-hoops cross) is lashed and other flexible green sticks are woven around the hoops so that they are parallel to the ground (start from the bottom and work upwards). Lash where each stick crosses another and place over-lapping broad leaves, bark or ferns from the bottom up so that rain will flow over:

A SMOKY FIRE just outside the door of the hut may offer some protection from insects

A "Pigmy hut"

OPEN FOREST: take advantage of patches of denser trees with low branches and rock outcrops with overhangs. Steep-sided dry creek banks may also afford some shelter but these can be dangerous due to sudden flooding.

For a more comfortable shelter, build a lean-to of sticks and tied bundles of grass which have been overlapped on the roof. CLEAR the ground of any dry grass and leaves before making a fire pit, remembering that there is more chance of a fire than in wetter forests.

OPEN GRASSLANDS - may have a greater range of temperature and insect pests, but all are usually windy. Seek rock shelters, groups of bushes or trees, dry creek beds (watch out for flash floods) or even natural dry hollows in the ground. Some added protection from wind may come from building a wall of sods of earth/grass (dig them out - about 40 cm. x 15 cm. x 10 cm.)

on the edge of a hollow. This is why having a small collapsible spade or trowel is important!

If possible, stretch a plastic sheet down from the top of this wall to the ground for some protection from rain (make a trench or drain around the outside of the hollow so that it does not fill with water. Line the floor with grass and take extra care of clearing a fire pit nearby:

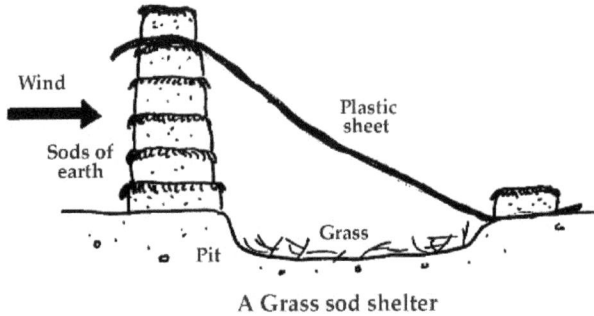

A Grass sod shelter

DESERTS - require protection from the sun during the day and from the cold at night (the best time to walk). It is vital to keep out of the sun in the middle of the day. Activity is best only two or three hours after sunrise and before sunset. These are the times for preparation.

Only experienced persons with the right gear should go into deserts. If stranded on a road, STAY with the vehicle!

Make use of whatever shade is available – rock overhangs, small thickets (dig a deep pit at their base on the side away from the sun) or dry stream beds (watch out for flash floods).

Make a low wall of rocks or hollow out a pit and pile the sand or dirt as a mound on the sunny side. If small trees are handy then one can use sticks as uprights in two corners or even cover the low plants with any cloth. Stretch a sheet of opaque material or any bushes from the top to the ground.

Do not attempt to burrow into the base of loose sand-dunes as these will collapse.

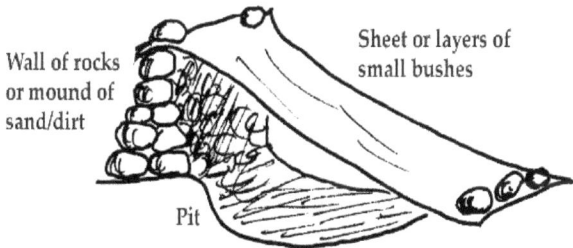

Wall of rocks or mound of sand/dirt

Sheet or layers of small bushes

Pit

MOUNTAINS AND SNOW - never try to walk at night in mountainous regions nor in snow in windy, cold conditions.

Always attempt to get below the tree-line and keep out of the wind (especially if wet – death from exposure will come quickly.)

Seek shelter in rocky outcrops (take care as snow drifts

may build up on the lee side as well) or where there are thick trees with low, branches touching the snow (if snow-laden, knock off the snow first).

If possible, build a small, personal fire on a flat pile of rocks or a raft of green, wet timber (scrape tinder from under tree bark, dry pine needles and use dead twigs from the lee side of trees - place a pile of bigger twigs which may be damp around the fire).

Under extreme conditions in the open, seek an old compact snow-drift and burrow into the base of the lee side. Dig horizontally into the drift and then upwards to form a small, rounded snow- cave. The entrance to the cave <u>must</u> be at the bottom or even through a small pit to trap the warm air. It may be sealed with a ball or cut slab of firm snow):

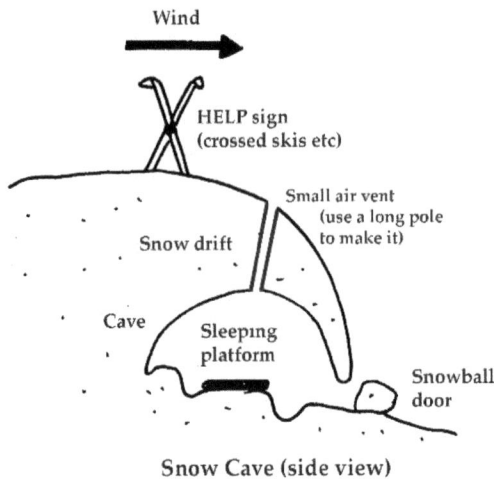

Snow Cave (side view)

To make the cave more effective:
- smooth of the inside walls to prevent drips;
- build the floor in three levels:
  UPPER LEVEL for dry storage;
  MIDDLE LEVEL with dry grass or branches (search at the base of bushy trees) for a raised sleeping platform; and
  LOWER LEVEL (below the level of the door) to trap cold air and melting water.
- if in a group, keep close together to save body heat - if the cold is extreme, share a sleeping bag with another below and the clothes on top;
- place a visible marker on top of the mound of snow - use a pole well-driven into the snow with a red/orange marker (strip of plastic, plastic cup etc.) on its top.

Some people suggest that a small fire or cooking stove may be used on flat rocks on the upper level. **Caution**! - there is a real danger of poisoning by carbon monoxide and other fumes. If cooking or a fire is used then a small ventilation hole must be poked through the ceiling but care should still be taken not to weaken the entire structure. It is probably better to make a small fire shelter for cooking, outside the door. As an extra precaution, it may be advisable to have a rostered watch kept throughout the night in case of a sudden temperature drop which may require all being awake and active.

7.6 Concluding Remarks
Shelter is very important in planning the trip and

potential emergency shelter should be considered before starting the trip. Even in places of mild climate, sudden changes can cause discomfort and even death by exposure if there is no shelter.

It is best if <u>everyone</u> has their own personal shelter (even a space blanket will do in emergencies). Tents and all their fittings should be checked by the owner before the trip – it is wrong to assume that everything is present and correct from the last trip.

After each trip, dry all equipment and repair or replace broken or missing fittings. If the tent has proven to be inadequate, discard it for a better model.

Chapter Eight: Ropes, Knots and Lashings

8.1 Taking Care of Ropes

Nylon and other man-made fibres are more resistant to water, rot, and insects and generally are preferred for most tasks. Nylon is also stronger and lighter but it will melt when hot (if near a fire or by too much friction on metal rings if abseiling etc.). It is also able to be snapped if bent over an edge.

Rope should be care for by:
- protecting it from any unnecessary heat, light and damp;
- drying wet rope naturally and not near a fire;
- not dragging the rope or leaving it in dirt or mud (grit will work in to the fibres) - a dirty rope can be washed in a stream but it must then be thoroughly dried;
- whipping the ends to stop it from fraying (see later); and
- using the rope for one intended purpose (do NOT use a climbing rope for any other task and keep a log of each time it was used).

8.2 Carrying Rope

When rope has to be stored or carried, it should be coiled properly so that there are no twists or sharp bends in it. Any knots should have been previously removed. Some methods of coiling rope are:

A SIMPLE COIL - make a coil about 40 centimetres in diameter by:

1. holding one end of the rope in one hand (bent at the elbow) whilst looping the rest of the rope over the partly opened hand, keeping each loop about the same size and parallel to the previous loop (the end held in the hand should also have a small length – about 20 cm. - folded back);
2. once all of the loops have been made, tightly wrap the free end around the strands of rope (including the small loop at the other end) - the wrapping moves from the open end of the small loop to near its end;
3. insert the loose end of the rope into the partly covered loop that is left and pull back on the other end of the rope to close the loop; and lastly
4. tie both free ends of the rope together.

A simple coil

A PLAITED ROPE - for a long rope that has to be carried through close timber or down rock faces where a coiled rope may be snagged, the length of rope is best plaited:

103

1. fold the rope in two by laying it along the ground or have another person help;
2. hold the closed end of the rope so that it makes a partial loop (twisting the entire end may help);
3. grasp the rope below this held loop and poke it through the loop with the other hand;
4. repeat this action (stretching the length out occasionally so that the rope does not twist) until all of the rope length has been used;
5. fold the plaited length over into a big loop and tie the loose ends to the last loop on the other end. Carry the plaited coil over the shoulder.

A plaited rope

If the plaited loop is still too long, un-plait the rope and fold it into four equal lengths instead of two and then re-plait it. A rope plaited in this fashion can be easily undone by undoing the tied coil, holding the loose ends and vigorously shaking the plait apart. Some climbers tie one end to an anchor point and throw the rest over a cliff, but there are problems with tangling if the rope has not been plaited correctly – practice is required!

8.3 Simple Knots

Sailors will often use the terms bends and hitches when referring to use of sheets (ropes to non-sailors).

A knot is that which is tied within a rope, a hitch ties a rope to another object like a hitching rail for horses or it might be a climbing carabiner or even another rope. A bend is a knot that joins two ropes together.

The standing end of a rope is the side or part of the rope that's not being used during knot tying. The working end is the side or part of the rope that is being used during knot tying.

Everyone should know these knots:

HALF HITCH - the simplest of all but not good as a stand-alone secure knot. It is more useful as a second knot to secure others (e.g. bowlines).

A half hitch

REEF KNOT (square knot) – used for tying two ropes of equal size together (but NOT Nylon as it will slip unless other knots are added).

A reef knot

FIGURE OF EIGHT KNOT – it is a good knot at the end of a rope so that the rope does not pull through an eye or pulley block and it is well-used by sailors:

Figure of eight knot

It can also be used as a basis for a secure knot around a peg or bar . This knot can be made by:

1. make a loose figure-of-eight knot with a good length at the free end;
2. pass this around the peg;
3. push the free end back into the <u>second</u> loop of the eight;
4. bring it around and over the top of the fixed end and back into the <u>first</u> loop and tighten.

Figure of eight around a peg

BOWLINE - the best knot for tying a rope around an object especially around the body when using a rope as a safety line. When using nylon rope, tie several half hitches as well and leave a plenty of spare rope at the loose end. To tie this knot:
1. put the rope around the object (or not, to make a loop) and make a small loop (hole) by passing the free end <u>over the top</u> of the rope;

2. bring the free end (the rabbit) around and up and out of the small loop;

3. then around the fixed end of the rope (the tree) and back down the small loop so that the free end is parallel to the rope of the big loop formed.

This is remembered by the ditty: **"The rabbit comes up from its hole, runs around the tree and goes back again".**

The bowline

For a waist loop around the body when it is used as a safety line or hauling someone up a cliff, thread the rope through the knot so that is <u>tight</u> around the body with the knot in front. Ensure that the knot is <u>not</u> under the diaphragm of the body (which will knock the wind out if there is a fall) and that there are at least <u>two</u> half hitches tied at the end with plenty of spare at the loose end.

To make a Running Bowline as a good SLIP knot, simply

pass the other (long) end of the rope through a bowline
and use the running loop thus formed:

A running bowline

All of these knots should be known instinctively –
practice with a small piece of rope whenever there is
spare time.

8.4 Other Knots and Hitches

A hitch is used when tying rope around another rope or
object. These include:

SHEET BEND - for joining two ropes (or sheets) of
different sizes but can also be used for joining ropes of
the same size:

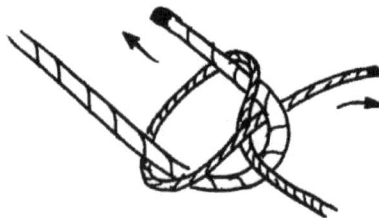

Sheet bend

DOUBLE SHEET BEND - even better for joining ropes, especially if they are wet:

Double sheet bend

FISHERMAN'S KNOT - another good join for wet ropes:

Fisherman's knot

BUTTERFLY (OR ARTILLERY) KNOT - excellent for making a loop in the middle of a rope (e.g. tying a body or object onto a climbing rope). To make this knot:

1. make a loop in the rope by turning the rope clockwise over the top of itself:

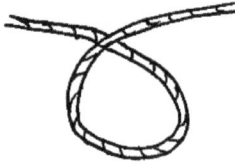

2. turn it over and allow the <u>left</u> side of the rope to hang over part of the loop:

3. twist the other part of the loop and pass this through between the hanging piece and the main rope. Pull it tight:

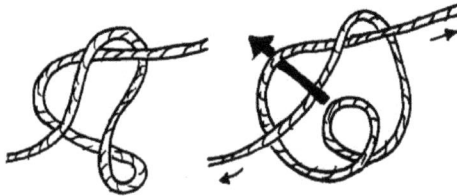

SHEEPSHANK - for shortening a rope. Never cut a rope unless it is really necessary. Fold the rope back onto itself to make three or more parallel lengths with loops on each end. Use the rope to tie half hitches around each loop.

Pull it tight.

Sheepshank

TRUCKIE'S KNOT - allows loads etc. to be well secured because the knot is tightened by pulling downwards. To make this knot:

1. make a loop in the rope by twisting anticlockwise and up;

2. make a small <u>bight</u> (a partial loop) below the small loop and bring it up through it – this will form a larger loop;

3. make a twist in this larger loop, run the end of the rope around the load and back up through this twist;

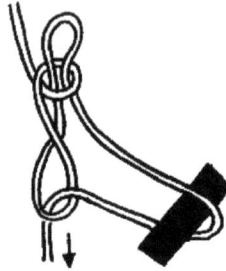

4. pull an end to tighten the knot - make several half
   hitches around the rope just to be sure.

PRUSIK KNOT - makes a slip knot on a larger rope which
only works when tension is removed. As soon as it is
pulled down, the knot stops on the rope.

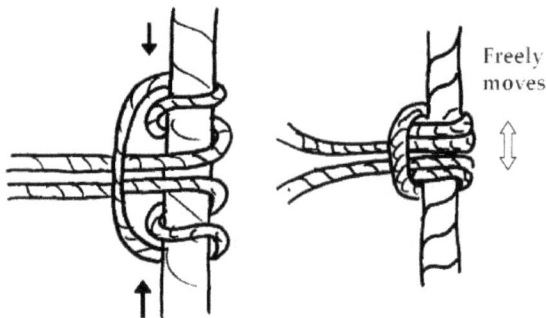

Freely
moves

Prusik Knot

Very useful in threes (with a bowline tied on the other
ends) for climbing up a long rope. These three Prusik
knots will have carabiners or bowline loops for two foot
loops and one bowline around the body's chest. Now

attached to the main rope, one walks up the rope by taking tension of one prussic and moves it up, then rest of that knot whilst another is pushed up and so on. **They are not good on frozen or wet ropes because there is less friction**.

weight holding

free

weight holding

Climbing using a Prusik knot system

TIMBER HITCH - makes a good hitch around logs when they need to be hauled:

Timber hitch

CLOVE HITCH - general purpose hitch when the strain is at right-angles to the log:

Clove hitch

8.5 Lashings

Lashing is used to tie objects such as poles together. They include:

SQUARE LASHING - tying poles at right-angles:

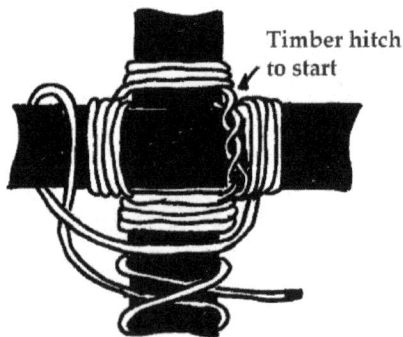

Timber hitch
to start

Square lashing

ROUND LASHING - to tie poles side-by-side:

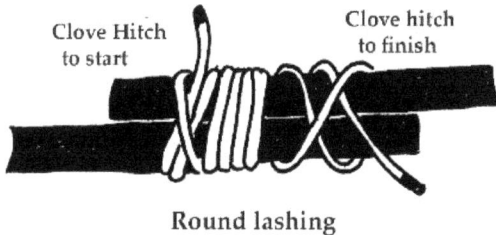

Round lashing

SHEAR LASHING - tying poles side-by-side so that they can be opened out to make an A-FRAME which can then have a third leg lashed (shear again) to make a tripod. Such a tripod is a very stable arrangement (SHEAR LEGS) and can be used as a support for a pulley to lift engines out of cars, transfer objects between two shear legs across a gulley or water or act as a simple support for a hanging pot over a cooking fire. To make a shear lashing:
1. tie a clove hitch around one SPAR (long pole);
2. lay the other spar next to the first and wrap rope (loosely) around both;
3. bring the loose end up between the spars and make several turns around the wrapping (and at right-angles to it);
4. tighten the lashing and finish with a clove hitch on the other end of the other spar:

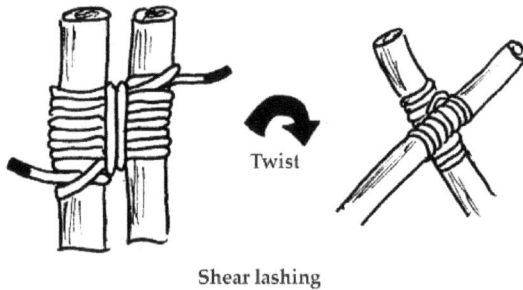

Twist

Shear lashing

8.6 Whipping a Rope

This is used to tie-off the ends of rope to stop it fraying, to secure and "streamline" splicing and to allow easy passage through pulleys. To make this lashing:

1. lay a length of strong twine along the rope so that it protrudes about 10-15 cm. past the end of the rope;

2. take the <u>other</u> end of the twine and start winding it ("Whipping") it around the rope tightly, starting about 2-3 cm. from the end and moving towards the end, stopping about halfway;

3. fold the other end of the twine back along its own

length so that it forms a loop. Continue whipping <u>over</u> this loop until the end of the rope is reached;

4. thread the end of the twine through this loop and pull on the <u>other</u> (loose) end of the twine to grab it;

5. cut off waste ends of twine and wrap with gaffer tape if you have some.

Pull and
cut excess

Chapter Nine: First Aid

9.1 Introduction

It is strongly recommended that those who regularly go into the field have <u>First Aid training</u> (see local Ambulance Officers). Considerable damage can be done by well-meaning but ill-informed persons undertaking what they think is first aid.

This chapter deals with only with the very basic first aid for some common problems encountered in the bush. Some techniques are outlined in case <u>only if there is no alternative.</u>

When confronted with an emergency:
- DON'T PANIC - take a minute to collect your thoughts;
- SEEK LOCAL, IMMEDIATE HELP but if no one else can act
- TAKE CHARGE if you are the best person for the job;
- SEND FOR HELP using a responsible person who will get help (if possible, send a party of 2 or 3). Write a message showing:
  LOCALITY (Latitude/Longitude if in
  wild country - not grid references),
  INJURY (symptoms - no guesses),
  BRIEF DETAILS AS NEEDED.
  (e.g. approaching danger, weather,
   problems with rest of party,
   water/food left...keep it brief!)

- USE OTHERS for assistance as required but get unwanted persons away from the injured – there may be some emotional stress so nominate a leader to keep the others away, quiet and BUSY (have a fire made and brew tea, build a shelter, clear an area for signals etc.)
- GET ON WITH THE JOB CALMLY (you can panic at home later! You can do your best now!)

Prevention is the best insurance against injury anticipate possible dangers before they happen during the entire trip (Whether you are the leader or not!)

Take all possible precautions but expect the unexpected.

Do not attempt to move casualties with suspected spinal injuries.

9.2 First Response

It is very important that one develops a **ROUTINE OF ACTION (ROA)** in case of an emergency. If first aid is not possible or there is a threat, remove the casualty from it and seek further aid. Such a routine could be:

1. Quickly check for immediate danger. This could be the cause of the emergency such as a dangerous animal, falling rocks, electrical cable etc. Remove the source of danger or the casualty from it;
2. Check the responsiveness of the casualty by gently shaking the casualty and speaking to them quietly

asking about the symptoms;

3. If there is no response then roll the casualty into the 'recovery position', check their airways and clear the mouth of any materials such as vomit, blood, false teeth. foreign objects etc. using the fingers;

The recovery position

4. **SEND FOR HELP IMMEDIATELY**

5. look, listen and feel for signs of breathing. If breathing continuously, check for bleeding and any change in the casualty. Do what you can to stop bleeding and make the casualty comfortable;

6. **if not breathing**, then open airway by supporting the jaw at the base of chin and lift it up and forward ensuring that pressure is not put on the neck. Give five (5) quick breaths to the casualty's mouth whilst holding the nose;

Open the airway

7. feel for a pulse by placing two of your fingers together on the Carotid Artery on the side of the neck or just left of centre on the wrist;

7. **if no pulse**, then give: Cardiopulmonary Resuscitation (C.P.R) if **trained** to do so. If untrained seek help from those nearby. If help is not immediately available then attempt C.P.R. with care (see below);

8. **If neither breath nor pulse, continue alternating between assisted breathing and chest compressions. Send for help immediately. If alone continue CPR/EAR WHILE YOU CAN.**

9.3 Cardiopulmonary Resuscitation (C.P.R)
If untrained, do not attempt C.P.R. unless there is no chance of help and it is the only alternative.

Finding no pulse:
1. **roll** the casualty onto his/her back and kneel at the side (level with the chest);
2. **expose** the casualty's chest or keep only a thin layer of

clothing on for females;

3. **locate** the centre of the chest by:
    a. finding the bottom of the breastbone by following the ribs up into the centre of the lower chest;
    b. finding the top of the breastbone by locating the groove between the collarbones (at the base of the neck);
    c. locate the position midway.

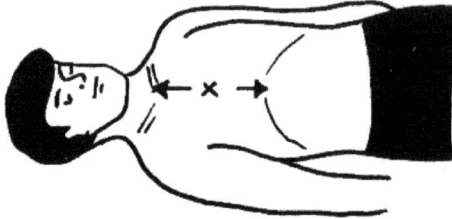

Finding the cenre of the chest

4. **place the palm of a hand** onto this mid-point so that the hand extends ACROSS the chest with the fingers relaxed and slightly raised;
5. **place the other hand** securely on top of the first by locking the thumb of it around the wrist of the lower hand, For BABIES, use only two finger tips and for YOUNG CHILDREN use only one hand:

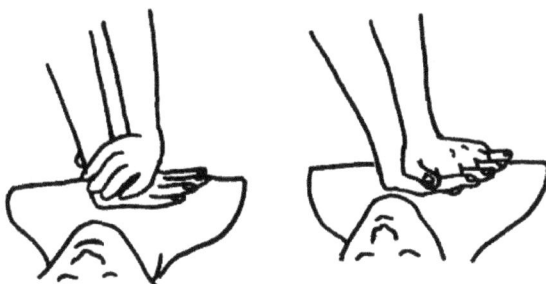

Hand positions

6. **exert pressure** using a straight arm and rocking motion from the hips just enough to depress the chest by about five centimetres (5 cm.) then relax by drawing back (for BABIES this compression should only be 1 to 2 cm. and for YOUNG CHILDREN about 2 to 3 cm.);
7. **give compressions at a rat**e of fifteen (15) every ten to twelve (10-12) seconds;
8. **after each15 compressions** give two breaths by mouth-to mouth over three to five (3-5) seconds; sing Stayin' Alive to yourself and keep the compressions to the beat.
9. **continue** this pattern at four cycles per minute (6 cycles per minute for children); and
10. **check for a pulse** every minute and STOP when one is felt.

9.4 Expired Air Resuscitation (E.A.R. or Mouth-to-Mouth) - unless there is a mouth injury or risk of serious infection, or you do not feel comfortable doing it.

Having cleared the airways and the casualty in the recovery position:

1. **roll** the casualty onto their back and kneel beside then level with their chest, preferably on their right side;
2. **tilt the head** back (NOT if the casualty is a baby) and lift the jaw to open the airway (do NOT put pressure on the neck) as before;
3. **take a medium breath** yourself, using a wide-open mouth;
4. **hold the casualty's nose** closed between forefinger and thumb;
5. **place your mouth** directly over that of the casualty to make a tight seal (with a small child you can cover both mouth and nose):
6. **breathe firmly** - but not too strongly; just enough to inflate the lungs (the chest will rise);
7. **remove your mouth** (but still hold their nose) and turn your head to observe the fall of the casualty's chest and listen for exhaled air (a good sign). If there is no fall, there may be an obstruction - roll the casualty onto their side an check and clear the airway as before
8. **continue** by giving FIVE (5) breaths in ten (10) seconds;
9. **check the pulse** at the Carotid Artery (as before – if no pulse go to CPR section 6.5 below) and if it exists then:
10. **continue E.A.R.** at a rate of 15 breaths per minute (20 smaller puffs per minute for children under 8) and continue to check the pulse regularly. Check to see if the casualty can breathe unassisted every 2 minutes.

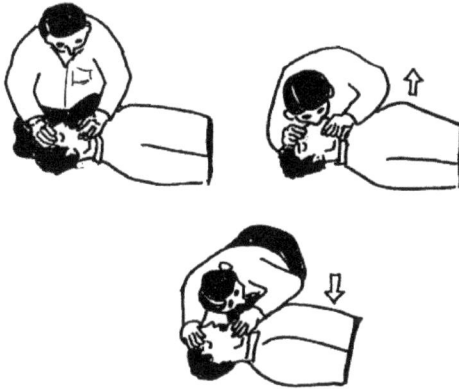

Performing Expired Air Resusitation

When breathing has returned - place in the recovery position

9.5 Specific Injuries (in alphabetical order) Many of the following problems are encountered when trekking. Whilst of a temporary nature, they must be treated as soon as possible otherwise more serious complications may occur.

Prevention is better than a cure

9.5.1 Abrasions - see Wounds and Abrasions

9.5.2Allergic Reaction
CAUSE: strong, personal body reaction to foreign chemicals such as in some foods, (e.g. nuts, caffeine, fish,

strawberries etc.) pollen, dust, some stings (plants & animals) and bites.

PREVENTION: be aware of your own allergies and those in the rest of the party and avoid areas or organisms which will cause the reaction.

Carry specific medication e.g. antihistamine and make sure that others in the party are aware of your allergy and the nature and location of any personal medication. Allergic reaction may also occur with certain common medicines (e.g. penicillin). Personal allergies should be noted in the front of this book.

SYMPTOMS: may vary depending on the reaction. Some symptoms may include swelling, change in breathing, sneezing, increased heart rate, sweating, coughing and lack of breath, nausea, faintness and collapse.

TREATMENT: remove the casualty from the source of irritation if possible, treat any wound, bite or rash in an appropriate manner.

Ask the casualty about any medication which they may have or can use e.g. antihistamine. A nasal wash with saltwater may stop excessive sneezing.

A very severe allergic reaction can lead to a condition called anaphylaxis, or **anaphylactic shock** resulting in confusion, vomiting and possibly collapse. In such cases ask the casualty if they have an EpiPen for use in such a severe case. Call 000 or local emergency number immediately.

Give E.A.R. or C.P.R. if absolutely necessary and seek medical attention in all cases.

9.5.3 Asthma Attack - many people are asthmatics and strenuous activity and cold air can be a problem.

CAUSE: sudden or progressive narrowing of airways so that the person cannot breathe. Panic often occurs. Attacks can be started by exercise, allergies, cold air, some artificial foods (especially preservatives), anxiety and stress, smoke and dust.

PREVENTION: know if you have this problem and to what extent of severity. Under supervision, exercise with good breathing technique (e.g. swimming).

Avoid major causes and do not be excessively active. Take extra precautions during spring and in cold or dusty/smoky conditions.

SYMPTOMS: severe breathing difficulties with wheezing and coughing. Paleness and sweating with blueness of lips and finger tips. May also be very quiet and lapse into unconsciousness.

TREATMENT: reassure and calm the casualty. Sit them upright. If they have appropriate medication (such as an inhaler), help them with it. Ensure fresh, warm air and encourage casualty to breath normally (cupping hands loosely over mouth and nose may help). Any severe asthma attack seek medical help immediately.

ROA if unconscious – seek medical help.

9.5.4 Bites and Stings

CAUSE: contact with biting and stinging animals and stinging plants (usually have broad leaves with fine hairs).

PREVENTION: keep the body covered when in areas

known to have potential danger especially in some seasons e.g. tick & mosquitoes.

Use insect nets at night. Wear insect repellent (place some around the tops of boots as well). Take care of hands and face when moving through scrub. Shake out boots before putting them on and take care when picking up rocks and logs.

TREATMENT: in general, remove the sting or clean the area and apply a cold pad (or cold, wet washer). Soothing bite creams may be of some use in reducing the irritation.

Watch for extreme symptoms such as excessive sweating, difficulty in breathing, excessive swelling, nausea, muscular weakness) which may indicate a very serious bite or **allergic reaction** (see 6.7). Call 000

9.5.5 Blisters

CAUSE: soft skin rubbing on wet/hard socks or other material. Often due to damp feet, perspiration or ill-fitting boots or loose equipment.

PREVENTION: keep feet dry; wear good boots (broken in before the trip); wear two pairs of woolen socks; change socks regularly (or turn inside out and swap feet); and avoid wrinkles or grass seeds etc. in socks.

TREATMENT: If small - wash, clean, air the skin and cover with a dressing (with a little antiseptic cream). If large – clean the area thoroughly. Cover with dressing with a little antiseptic cream.

9.5.6 Bruises

CAUSE: due to impact from falls, blows or crushing. Some allergic reactions may also cause bruises. Bruises are caused by bleeding under/in the skin within the deep tissues often with pain and swelling.

PREVENTION: take care when walking and climbing to avoid falls and impact.

TREATMENT: rest the casualty, especially the injured part which should be elevated. Cool the bruise by contact (ice packs ideal but frozen food packs, snow or cool compresses will do but remember to wrap cold objects in a towel or cloth first) for twenty (20) minutes every two hours in the first day and every four hours thereafter until the bruise goes down.

9.5.7 Burns and Scalds

CAUSE: carelessness with cooking fires and pots; bush fires; rope burns; electrical and chemical burns.

PREVENTION - take care with fires and use tongs or cloth to pick up hot objects. Never handle fuels near naked flame and never throw liquid fuel onto fires (label bottles so that they are not mistaken for water bottles!). Carry hot water cans low to the ground.

TREATMENT: hold under cold water for at least FIFTEEN MINUTES (in a stream or cover lightly with a loose, wet cloth kept wet). Allow to dry in air and cover with a dry, non-stick, lint-free dressing. If pain persists, pour water over dressing. Seek medical attention immediately if severe (deep or larger than a 20c coin) or of airways or genitals, hand (extensive) or face. **Do not** apply lotions, give alcohol to drink, suddenly cool the area with extreme cold (causing shivering) nor use adhesive or fluffy dressings and cloth on the burn. (See also SUNBURN).

9.5.8 Choking

CAUSE: foreign matter in windpipe e.g. laughing or crying or falling whilst eating and drinking. Lack of chewing when eating. Swallowing bone. Inhaling whilst eating or drinking.

PREVENTION: sensible eating and drinking habits. Do not eat nor drink too fast. Chew thoroughly.

SYMPTOMS: violent coughing and attempts to breathe. Blueness to the face and collapse with breathing absent.

TREATMENT: <u>if conscious,</u> calm the casualty and encourage them to cough. Put the head down by bending over (Children may be held upside down but well supported around body (NOT by the feet). Give three (3) or four (4) sharp blows with the palm of the hand between the shoulder blades (Not too hard with young children!). Seek medical attention if airways not completely clear.

<u>If unconscious,</u> try to remove any obstruction from the mouth. Treat as above and apply E.A.R. when obstruction is removed.

9.5.9 Concussion

CAUSE: sudden blow to the head or sudden rapid movement of the head.

PREVENTION: care when walking, especially on rocky

surfaces. Wear protective helmet if climbing, caving, cycling or canoeing.

SYMPTOMS: loss of short-term memory (ask the casualty simple questions e.g. their name, what happened etc.), headache, disorientation, nausea, blurring of vision, pupils becoming unequal in size. Dizziness and collapse. Effects may be delayed well after the blow to the head so watch any person who has suffered a head injury.

Care: spinal injuries may have occurred following a head injury with unconsciousness! Keep casualty immobile, warm and seek medical attention.

TREATMENT: **ROA**

Turn casualty onto the injured side (support head and neck), check and clear the airway, control any bleeding with a light dressing on the wound. Do not apply any direct pressure to the skull in case of a possible fracture - some deformation may show).

SEEK MEDICAL HELP IMMEDIATELY.

9.5.10 Diabetes
Low blood sugar (Hypoglycaemia)

CAUSE: not enough blood sugar. This may be due to too much insulin (naturally produced or too much injected) or simply by too much exercise or not enough food.

PREVENTION: good habits in eating without overdoing exercise. Have many small snacks on the trip. If using insulin, do not overdo it. Make a note of your need in the front of this book and tell others in the party.

SYMPTOMS: paleness and blueness around lips and fingertips (under fingernails). Feeling of weakness and fainting, possible collapse. Sweating and hunger with rapid pulse. Mental confusion, possibly aggressiveness.

TREATMENT: give glucose tablets or sugary drink (e.g. soft drink, cordial but NO alcohol) or normal food. Continue giving drink every fifteen (15) minutes.

If unconscious – give nothing by mouth and **ROA - seek medical help if serious.**

High blood sugar (hyperglycaemia)

CAUSE: infection or insufficient insulin in a diabetic. Too much blood sugar in body. Dehydration.

PREVENTION: maintain normal dosages of insulin. Drink water in small doses regularly. Exercise.

SYMPTOMS: excessive thirst and need to urinate. Hot dry skin, rapid pulse, smell of acetone on the breath (like nail polish remover), drowsiness and finally unconsciousness.

TREATMENT: If conscious, allow the casualty to self-administer insulin. give sugar-free fluids and foods. **ROA immediately seek medical help.**

9.5.11 Dislocation of joints

CAUSE: sudden movement or stretching and bending of joints, especially in fingers, wrists, knees or shoulder.

PREVENTION: care in movement, specially involving the shoulders and wrists.

SYMPTOMS: excessive pain, deformity and swelling of the particular joint.

TREATMENT: do NOT attempt to reset the position of the dislocated joint.

Pack around with soft padding such as spare clothing and immobilize with a splint on legs and a sling for shoulders, elbows and wrist. Apply cold compress to reduce swelling and stop any bleeding with a light dressing.

SEEK MEDICAL HELP.

9.5.12 Drowning
CAUSE: water in the airways and lungs.
PREVENTION: care when entering unknown waterways and know your limitations. Always watch small children constantly (whether or not in your care) and watch non-swimmers. Wear buoyancy vests when canoeing or boating. Care when fording running water and around the edges of muddy lakes.
SYMPTOMS: no breathing, blue face or lips, possibly no pulse.
TREATMENT: Safely remove casualty from the water (or seek help if this is beyond your capabilities). Follow full E.A.R. procedures (C.P.R. also if no pulse).
ROA - seek urgent medical help.

9.5.13 Epilepsy
CAUSE: seizure triggered by brain pattern
disruption. May be induced by over excitement and flickering light such as sunlight through moving leaves, strobe lamps etc. in susceptible people.
PREVENTION: over excitement and flickering lights should be avoided by known epileptics who should let others know of their condition (fairly common situation

usually without major problem.)

SYMPTOMS: person suddenly falls (sometimes with a slight cry) and lies rigid with body arched for a short time. This may be followed by jerking, frothing at the mouth and perhaps loss of bladder or bowel control.

Seizure may be violent. After the attack, the person will awake and be unaware of what has happened. They will be confused and very tired.

TREATMENT: protect the casualty from injury without restricting their movement. Move nearby objects which may cause injury and calm onlookers. Do not attempt to put objects in the mouth.

Treat injuries caused by the seizure and wait until they awake. Give calm reassurance and allow the casualty to sleep. **Seek medical help if the seizure lasts longer than ten (10) minutes.**

9.5.14 Fainting

CAUSE: fatigue by too much exertion, especially if the body is too hot. Person becomes weak, giddy, irrational, suffers nausea and headache.

PREVENTION: wear appropriate loose, light-weight clothing in summer. Do not exert oneself (or others) and have regular short rests in shade. Drink plenty of water.

Walk and work in the cool of the day or under shade whenever possible.

TREATMENT: remove the casualty to a cool, shady place, loosen clothing and allow to rest with head down and legs raised. Apply a cool (not cold) compress on the forehead. Give a little cool water when recovered.

9.5.15 Fractures (Broken Bones)

CAUSE: direct force due to blows or falls.

PREVENTION: extra care when walking or climbing, especially on bad surfaces and if elderly.

SYMPTOMS: deformity, inability to move limb, pain, swelling, bruising. Bleeding internally or externally if it is a **compound fracture**. Permanent tissue damage and shock may occur.

TREATMENT: control bleeding, immobilize casualty and the fractured part by using a splint (any rigid material) or by strapping to the rest of the body (e.g. strap a fractured leg to the good leg). Do not dry to reset the position of the broken bone. Place a cool compress over the injured part. SEEK MEDICAL HELP.

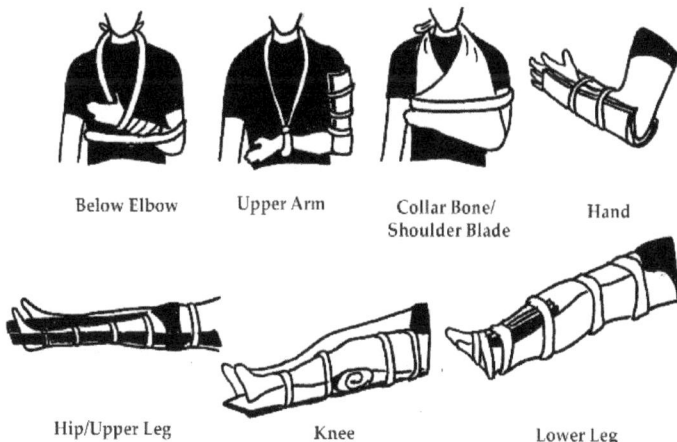

Below Elbow   Upper Arm   Collar Bone/
Shoulder Blade   Hand

Hip/Upper Leg   Knee   Lower Leg

Some immobilization techniques

9.5.16 Head Injuries - treat as per Concussion.

SEEK MEDICAL HELP IMMEDIATELY.

9.5.16 Headache

CAUSE: too much heat and light glare. Lack of body fluids and other causes such as restricted blood vessels in the surface skin of the head.

PREVENTION: wear loose and light clothing in hot weather, including a broad-brimmed hat. Ensure that hats are not tightly fitting. Sun glasses may be worn if there is intensive light. Drink plenty of water.

TREATMENT: lie down and rest with a cool compress on the affected part of the head. If the casualty has medication, they may take it, if symptoms persist seek medical aid.

9.5.17 Heat Exhaustion

CAUSE: hot conditions and lack of water which causes loss of body fluids and salts by excessive perspiration. Too much clothing.

PREVENTION: keep cool and drink frequently - many small amounts are better than few big amounts. There is no need to take salt tablets. Wear light clothing over all of the body and wear a broad-brimmed hat.

SYMPTOMS: faintness, headache, vomiting, cramps, much sweating (but cool, pale skin), rapid breathing.

TREATMENT: rest with head down in the shade. Cool the head and upper body with a wet cloth and fan. Give water (perhaps with a **little** salt - pinch to a cup) a little at a time and continue at intervals.

Seek medical help. It can turn to Heat Stroke in minutes.

9.5.18 Heat Stroke - is life threatening!
CAUSE: untreated heat exhaustion. Too much heat too quickly. Can occur near large fires.
PREVENTION: keep away from extreme heat such as wildfires or retreat as required.
SYMPTOMS: sweating stops giving a dry and sensitive skin, flushed appearance, mental confusion, poor coordination, full pulse and noisy breathing, sudden collapse.
TREATMENT: move casualty into shelter away from heat radiation. Sponge the skin until normal body temperature is regained and if conscious, give water a little at a time.
CPR and EAR if required.

SEEK MEDICAL HELP IMMEDIATELY.

9.5.19 Hypothermia
From exposure to extreme cold, especially if wet. Even in countries with a mild or hot climate, there will be times when sudden reduction of temperature will cause death by sudden loss of body heat within minutes e.g.in the mountains in summer, the weather can change to sleet within minutes. Be aware of possible changes in weather when venturing into mountainous regions or in winter.
CAUSE: sudden loss of body heat due to low outside temperatures.

PREVENTION: always go prepared for colder and wetter weather. Extra care should be taken in high, colder regions where snow could fall in summer. Know a route out if caught in bad weather. **Always** carry spare jacket and rain gear on any trip.

SYMPTOMS: body will feel cold, feeling of weakness disorientation and panic. Slow pulse, shallow breathing and a period of disinterest (food may be refused) followed by unconsciousness.

TREATMENT: remove casualty to a warm but not hot place. Place them between blankets (or partially stripped with a friend in a sleeping bag) and give warm drinks if conscious. Watch for shock and lapses of consciousness. If unconscious watch for failure of breathing and lack of pulse and only give resuscitation if there is absolutely no pulse). Do not use hot baths or water bottles.

SEEK MEDICAL AID IMMEDIATELY

9.5.20 Internal Bleeding
CAUSE: due to sudden impact or a fall with damage of internal organs and tissues.

PREVENTION: general care when walking and climbing. Padding and helmet as appropriate.

SYMPTOMS: coughing-up frothy blood (from lungs), vomiting blood (from stomach/intestines), red urine (from kidneys), red bowel motions (from lower digestive tract) or general tenderness, pain and rigidity of stomach muscles (bleeding in the abdomen).

Also: faintness, nausea, thirst, weak but rapid pulse, cold clammy skin, rapid breathing and pallor.

TREATMENT: lay the casualty down with raised legs or at least bent knees unless they are coughing/ vomiting then allow to half sit.

Reassure the casualty. Give nothing by mouth.

SEEK MEDICAL HELP URGENTLY.

9.5.21 Leeches

CAUSE: walking in damp forests or swamps infested with leeches which will cause much bleeding, especially inside boots (they inject an anticoagulant), and perhaps some infection.

PREVENTION: avoid swampy conditions and walking in rain if possible; tuck trousers into socks and ensure laces are well tied. Spray or rub insect repellent around ankles (outside on socks). Check feet, necks and backs regularly.

TREATMENT: If observed e.g. if feet feel very slippery, remove boots or other item of clothing, sprinkle salt or apply a hot match to the leech to make it drop off. Never pull the leech off directly. Allow some blood to flow for a short time to remove infection and treat as a minor wound.

9.5.22 Poisoning

CAUSE: ingesting contaminated food or water. Drinking fuel by error. Eating the wrong wild foods. Skin contact with plant, animal and other absorbed toxins.

PREVENTION: care with foods and water. Never drink from streams unless they are clear and running. Never drink water containing blue-green algae. Label all FUEL bottles clearly. Do not eat spoiled food and be very careful with wild foods – even the experts have been poisoned!

SYMPTOMS: pains and/or burning sensation in mouth or stomach or on the part poisoned. Nausea and discolouration of lips or skin. Vomiting. Swelling of affected skin and difficulty in breathing.

TREATMENT: Check to see that the symptoms were not caused by a bite or sting (puncture marks or barb). If conscious, ask the casualty what they have recently swallowed

Contact POISONS INFORMATION 131126 follow their directions.

If poisoned through the skin by contact (e.g. by touching poisonous plants and some animals), wash the area and clothing with much water and treat any injury as a burn.

SEEK MEDICAL HELP IMMEDIATELY.

9.5.23 Shock

CAUSE: any distress or massive injury especially loss of blood and body fluid. Heart damage.

PREVENTION: reduce the chance of massive trauma and blood loss.

SYMPTOMS: may be delayed after injury and develop progressively. After any injury watch for symptoms such as pale clammy skin, pale fingernails and lips, weak, rapid pulse with rapid breathing. Faintness and nausea, restlessness and thirst in some cases may also occur.

TREATMENT: **ROA** and control any bleeding. Reassure the casualty, raise legs slightly (unless fractured) and loosen tight clothing. Keep the casualty warm but not hot. Do not give liquids (moisten lips if thirsty). Place them on their side if there is breathing difficulty.

SEND FOR MEDICAL HELP IMMEDIATELY.

9.5.24 Snake Bite - usually rare

CAUSE: accidental contact with snake or picking one up (**stupid**!).

PREVENTION: make some noise when walking through grass and watch where you are walking or climbing. Choose seasons when snakes are not active such as winter. Wear good boots, thick socks and tough long trousers in vegetated country. Never put arms into ground holes or dead trees and do not try to pick up nor kill snakes (they are faster than you!). Seal up tents, pack away clothing and roll up sleeping bags when not in use. Check boots, clothing, bedding and tents before using.

SYMPTOMS: often the bite (and possibly) the snake (try to make a quick identification) will be seen. There will be pain for all snakebites, but venomous bites may also cause nausea, faintness, cramps, breathing difficulties, double vision, rapid pulse, tightness in the chest and loss of consciousness (after from fifteen minutes to two hours).

TREATMENT: **ROA**. Keep the casualty still and apply a widely taped pressure bandage over the bite. If on a limb, cover the bite area and continue below with a constrictive pressure bandage then wind the bandage round and above the bite. Do not use a string, tie, rope or narrow bandage, it must be wide. Do not allow the casualty to move. Do NOT wash off venom (use it for identification). Do NOT cut nor suck the wound. Do NOT try to kill nor catch the snake.

SEEK MEDICAL HELP IMMEDIATELY.

9.5.25 Spider Bites - rarely fatal
CAUSE: venom injected into bloodstream after bite.
PREVENTION: Do not put hands in holes or in tree hollows. Watch carefully when climbing trees, rocks and near old fences or in old sheds. Take care when gathering firewood. Wear good boots and cover the legs. Shake out any clothing or sleeping gear before use. Shake out boots before putting them on (don't use the fingers for checking boots etc.).
SYMPTOMS: for most spider bites there will be a sharp pain. For dangerous spiders there may also be nausea, swelling, sweating and muscular weakness.
In addition, some spiders give other symptoms e.g. **Funnel Web Spiders** cause weeping from eyes, cold skin and shivering, and coughing-up mucus. **Red Back Spiders** (Black Widows in the US) also cause rapid pulse and dizziness).
TREATMENT: **ROA if severe**. Reassure the casualty and apply a cold compress on the area. For **Funnel Webs only** - apply a pressure bandage around the area of the wound (as with snake bite).
SEEK MEDICAL HELP IMMEDIATELY.

9.5.26 Splinters and Thorns
CAUSE: contact with broken timber and thorny plants.

PREVENTION: cover exposed parts (do not walk with bare feet, arms nor legs in scrub). Watch what you handle. Often one does not notice small thorns and splinter until they become infected.

TREATMENT: remove with clean needle or forceps (a magnifying glass is handy). Treat as a wound. If it is too large or if there is deep and dangerous penetration (especially to the eye), cover with a clean dressing and seek help.

9.5.27 Sprains

CAUSE: twisting ankle or arm during a fall which may damage ligaments and tissues of the joint which swells and causes pain and inability to move the joint.

PREVENTION: care when walking or climbing. Always watch where the next foot will be placed. Wear good boots with firm ankle support.

TREATMENT: for the usual simple sprain, remove the boot, swelling is likely. Rest, wrap a supporting bandage firmly but make sure you can put your finger between the bandage and ankle. Use ice packs wrapped in a towel for 20 minutes on, 2 hours off. Elevate the leg.

Serious sprains are dangerous - keep the casualty still and seek assistance.

9.5.28 Sunburn

CAUSE: over exposure to ultra-violet rays from the sun. This can also occur in cold areas with ice and snow and on the water with extra reflection off the surface giving severe burns underneath eyes, chin, and ears. Sunburn can also occur when the sky is overcast. Fifteen minutes (less for fair skin) is enough.

PREVENTION: cover the skin with loose fitting clothing (cotton is best - long sleeved shirt and pants) and broad-brimmed hat. Use 30+ blockout cream on exposed surfaces such as face, neck (especially its back) and tops of hands. Reapply often.

TREATMENT: keep the area cool by bathing it or use a wet compress, drink plenty of water and seek medical help if the burn is severe with many big blisters (especially if on a child).

9.5.29 Ticks

CAUSE: ticks are found in scrub in hotter months and may drop from above. They will try to burrow into the skin especially in moist area or folds (e.g. behind the ear, under armpits, in groin. Infection may result, especially if part of the tick is left in the body.

PREVENTION: in tick areas, tuck trousers into socks and roll collars over. Check body each night, especially if one has a drowsy and nauseous feeling.

TREATMENT: search and locate the tick (seen as a small brown, circular or oval body with small legs partly dug into the skin. Remove **all** of the tick (especially its head using fine tweezers by squeezing their ends around and deep into the skin around the head. If the tick is very deep, make it back out by applying a drop of alcohol or gently rubbed soft soap. Then treat as a small wound.

9.5.30 Vomiting and diarrhoea

CAUSE: eating or drinking contaminated food and water. Allergic reaction to bites, stings and foreign matter. Effects of the heat. Poor hygiene.

PREVENTION: care with foods and water. Protection from heat. Washing hands and utensils before food preparation. A bottle of water with disinfectant and a little detergent can be used to wash hands or use sanitizing liquid where water is scarce).

Excessive vomiting and diarrhoea are dangerous due to the rapid loss of fluids and dehydration.

SYMPTOMS: casualty vomiting repeatedly over short time or complaining of diarrhoea. Frequent trips to the latrine.

TREATMENT: ensure that the casualty replaces body fluids regularly. Give regular sips of water with a little salt and sugar added (one teaspoon of each to one litre of boiled water which has been cooled).

Rest and calm the casualty.

SEEK MEDICAL HELP IF EXCESSIVE

9.5.31 Wasp (European)

CAUSE: multiple attacks possible and injection of venom.

PREVENTION: keep well covered and do not interfere with wasps nor their nests. Seek shelter in a tent if attacked.

SYMPTOMS: extreme pain, swelling, difficulty in breathing if stung in the throat or mouth.

TREATMENT:

Wash the area and apply a cold compress.

Watch for allergic reaction. ROA and seek medical help if needed.

9.5.32 Wounds and Abrasions

CAUSE: carelessness with sharp or pointed objects including sharp rocks, plants, knives and broken glass. Falling onto hard surfaces.

PREVENTION: take care when moving. Prevent falls and resulting cuts and abrasions by walking on stable ground. When passing through a fence, have one person hold barbed wire apart whilst the others pass through. Care with sharp objects such as knives.

TREATMENT: wash the wound thoroughly using very weak saltwater (one teaspoon to a cup of water) or weak antiseptic solution (make fresh as per instructions on bottle). Dry the wound in air and cover with a lint-free dressing held by non-allergenic plaster tape.

Major wounds with excessive amounts of blood loss may need a pressure bandage over and around the wound (no tourniquets!). If possible, raise the injured part above the level of the heart.

Seek help if the wound is large and deep. If bleeding cannot be stopped, especially if from an artery which spurts out, apply a firm bandage around the wound. Treat for shock.

9.6 Carrying an Injured Person - see Chapter 12 : Communications and Rescue

9.7 The First Aid Kit

Every person should have a small personal first aid kit and some simple medical items should also be in their emergency kit. It is highly recommended that everyone venturing into the wild be First Aid trained.

Professional first aid kits containing all the necessities can be purchased from St. John's Ambulance, Red Cross or other reputable first aid authorities.

People with special medical needs must ensure that they are carrying fresh personal medication which should be well-labelled, documented (see the front of this book) and be easily located in case others have to look for it. Others of the party, especially any leader should be aware of these needs and with children, it is a good idea for the leader or a designated adult to collect and document specific medications.

For most simple trips lasting only a few days, the first aid kit needs to be small but packed in a strong, water-proofed box (e.g. small plastic lunch box). This should be sealed with gaffer tape (always useful!) and always checked and restocked before the next trip (some medicines do not keep long). It should contain:

- adhesive dressing strips (non-allogenic)
- sterile dressings (several sizes-small and large)
- alcohol swabs – sealed in packets
- gauze squares
- surgical gloves, resuscitation mouth piece
- cotton wool swabs
- triangular bandages (2)
- crepe roller bandage (2)
- adhesive plaster /Micropore tape
- corn plasters (small/round) (for personal use)
- butterfly sutures for larger wounds
- safety pins (several - medium and large)
- small scissors or scalpel blade (sharp)
- fine forceps (tweezers)
- needle (medium size and sharp) (for personal use)
- magnifying lens (small)
- paracetamol tablets for headache and pain relief. (for personal use)
- asthma puffer (for personal use)
- antihistamine tablets (for personal use)
- antiseptic cream in a tube (for personal use)
- calamine lotion or other anti-sting cream (for personal use)
- Condy's crystals (potassium permanganate)
- salt in sachets
- matches (small book type)

NOTE ANY CREAMS OR MEDICATIONS ARE FOR PERSONAL USE ONLY UNLESS YOU ARE A DOCTOR IT IS ILLEGAL TO USE THEM ON OTHERS

In addition, one should also take sunburn cream (30+ blockout), insect repellent in a roll on (not aerosol), and water sterilizing tablets (although Condy's crystals may do but water will be pink).

Chapter Ten: Navigation

10.1 Introduction

It is very important that all who go hiking have some idea of:

- knowing where they are;
- where they are going; and
- how to get there.

As well as being an enjoyable exercise, persons other than the leader should know the details of the navigation of the trip in case they are needed to continue or modify the trip should the navigator be injured.

GPS and other electronic aids are excellent but they may not be able to get a good signal in some places, can easily be damaged and are sometimes subject to error. It is therefore a good idea to learn the basics of navigation using the traditional methods. The basic tools of Navigation are:

- the MAP (which should be supplemented with an up-to-date aerial photographs);
- a good (fluid-filled) compass which should be of the prismatic type or equivalent;
- a 360^0 protractor (good, clear type);
- a ruler, pencils and eraser; and
- a piece of fine string (such as a long lanyard on the compass)
- a small map envelope to carry the map during rain is also very useful (old British Army map cases are

excellent) as are chinagraph pencils for writing on plastic.

10.2 The Map

A map is a two-dimensional representation of the three-dimensional land surface at the time when data for it was compiled. Maps sometimes are inaccurate in so much that they may:

- generalize the land surface (e.g. flat country may be riddled with gullies);
- not show all the detail (a scale may be left off);
- be out of date (e.g. the roads have been changed); or
- simply contain vague or wrongly plotted information (look for the reliability diagram near the bottom of the map which shows its accuracy level).

A good map should clearly show:

- its name and sheet series;
- its location on a wider scale (including adjoining maps);
- a scale - as a fraction (e.g. 1:25,000) and as a linear scale (like a ruler);
- latitude and longitude (at least two lines of each);
- a grid system of reference;
- clear contour lines showing heights (with well-defined contour intervals - smaller the better);
- magnetic declination (variation) diagram showing True North, Grid North, Magnetic North and the Magnetic Declination (and its change each year);
- reliability diagram to show the accuracy of parts of the map; and

- a legend of conventional symbols.

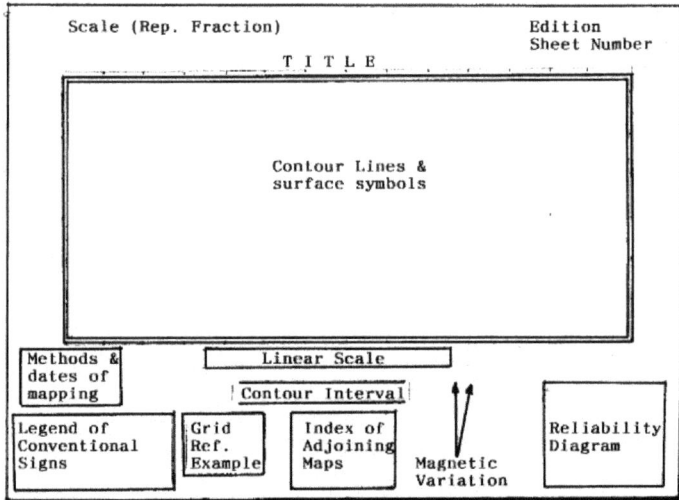

A typical topographical (survey) map

10.3 Caring for the Map

Maps usually do not last long if exposed to the weather. They can be water-proofed with spray-on liquids but do not use any which makes the map rigid and unable to be folded. It is best if the map is:

- folded the same way each time;
- carried in a plastic envelope or bag;
- never used completely open in a wind (fold so that only the appropriate section is open);
- stored in a flat pouch in the pack (often in the top flap) or in a wide pocket;

- written upon with a pencil rather than biro. In rain or snow, keep the map in the plastic
- pocket and use chinagraph pencils on the outside of the plastic envelope;
- kept away from food, water and sunshine when not being used.

All maps must be up-dated whenever mistakes are found - make direct changes to old maps or buy a new edition (but check that this is accurate!)

10.4 Map Scales

These are usually given as:

a representative fraction e.g. 1:25,000 which means that one unit measured directly on the map (e.g. from a 1:25,000 map, one centimetre on the map represents twenty-five thousand centimetres = 250 metres on the ground).

Bigger scaled maps (e.g. 1:100,000) represent a bigger area and longer distances and are more difficult for local hiking (e.g. for 1:100,000, 1 cm. = 1000 metres).

Linear scale (given as a line divided into measured divisions). This is the most useful form of scale for quickly finding distance. The actual distance on the map is measured by placing a ruler (along straight features or as-the-crow-flies) or a piece of fine string (e.g. a bootlace) between the two points concerned then this is matched up against the linear scale.

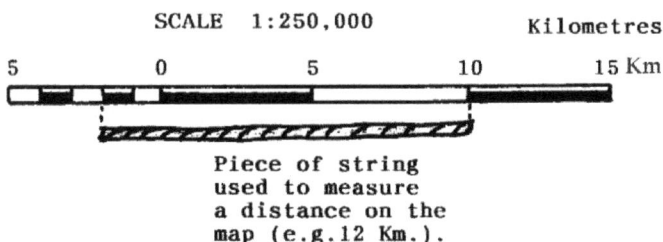

SCALE   1:250,000   Kilometres

5   0   5   10   15 Km

Piece of string
used to measure
a distance on the
map (e.g.12 Km.).

Measuring on a linear scale

Remember that distance measured on the map represents the direct distance between two points as though they were on <u>flat</u> ground. you must take into account that most land is not flat.

10.5 Estimating Distance and Angles

A rough way of estimation of the distance to a visible object from sight to check the map is to use a simple method of triangulation. To do this:

1. select a good, visible reference point at your current position (e.g. tree, marker left on a tree or another person);
2. take a compass bearing (described later in this chapter) to the distant object;
3. turn exactly 90^0 from this bearing (you can use the compass by adding 90^0 to the first bearing) and march out a set number of paces (e.g. 10 paces - but longer is better<u>) in a straight line </u>to a position where the distant

object can still be seen;

4. take a second bearing to the distant object;
5. subtract or add the bearings to get the difference (very distant objects will only be a very small angle, so use a longer set of paces):

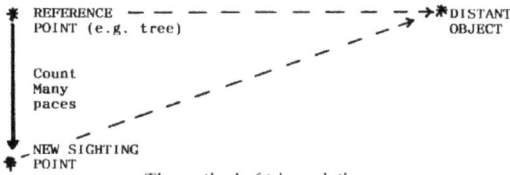

The method of triangulation

6. subtract this bearing difference from ninety;
7. refer to the following table (of Tangents) for the appropriate multiplying factor to use with your measured baseline.

ANGLE	FACTOR	ANGLE	FACTOR	ANGLE	FACTOR
6 5	2 . 1	7 3	3 . 3	8 1	6 . 3
6 6	2 . 2	7 4	3 . 5	8 2	7 . 1
6 7	2 . 4	7 5	3 . 7	8 3	8 . 1
6 8	2 . 5	7 6	4 . 0	8 4	9 . 5
6 9	2 . 6	7 7	4 . 3	8 5	1 1 . 4
7 0	2 . 7	7 8	4 . 7	8 6	1 4 . 3
7 1	2 . 9	7 9	5 . 1	8 7	1 9 . 1
7 2	3 . 1	8 0	5 . 7	8 8	2 8 . 6
				8 9	5 7 . 3

For example: a tree on the far side of a stream has a compass bearing of 180^0 (i.e. south) from your position. At 90^0 to this bearing (e.g. due west at 270^0) and ten paces away, the new bearing to the tree is now 177^0. How wide is the stream?

The difference in angle is 180^0-177^0 or three degrees

Subtract this from Ninety = eighty-seven degrees.

Refer to table gives a factor of: 19.1

Multiply by number of paces of your baseline (e.g. 10 paces) = 19.1 x 10, so the stream is roughly 190 paces wide.

You should be able to convert paces to metres by knowing how many of your paces make exactly 100 metres from a measurement taken at home (on a 100 m athletic track or pool). The average for a normal-sized person is 120 paces = 100 metres on <u>flat</u> ground)

If you do not have a compass - hand angles can be used to obtain the final angle (i.e. that used in the table) but a much longer baseline is needed.

An outstretched hand (male adult) when the arm is fully extended is used to estimate angles using:

- between two knuckles (=3^0)

- all knuckles (= 8^0)

- out-stretched fingers, no thumb (=12^0)

- fully, out-stretched hand (=19^0)

You should determine <u>your own</u> hand angle by extending the arm and hand so that the tip of the thumb is aligned with a distant reference point (e.g. obvious tree) and another which can be seen beyond the tip of the small finger. The body is rotated on the spot, moving the thumb now to the small finger's reference point and so on until one complete turn (back to the first reference point) has been made. Divide 360 degrees by the number of hand spans taken for one circle.

10.6 Representing Height on a Map

Maps attempt to show three-dimensional surfaces or relief on a flat two-dimensional sheet. This can be done by simply using shading (not very useful) and spot heights. These are isolated heights given for particular spots, such as hilltops - usually it will be shown by a small triangle or trig. Point and a height or it may be given as a bench mark - a flat section part way up a slope - indicated by B.M. and a height.

The best maps indicate heights and surface shapes using contour lines. Contour lines are curved lines which join places of equal height above (mean) sea level. More recent maps will have the contour lines and their contour interval (the representative vertical height between any two adjacent contour lines) given in metres. The contour interval will be stated clearly on the map, usually near a corner or near the linear scale, or one can see it by comparing the heights of two close contour lines.

One should know how to identify certain topographical (land surface) features simply by their contour patterns as seen from above (i.e. looking on the map):

Remember:

- the closer the contour lines are together, the steeper is the slope;
- gullies and ridges which are less than the contour interval will not be shown – use aerial photographs for such detail.

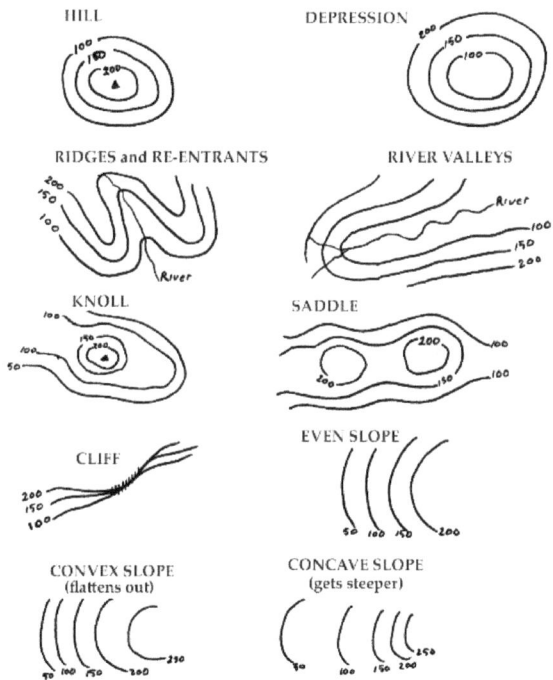

HILL

DEPRESSION

RIDGES and RE-ENTRANTS

RIVER VALLEYS

KNOLL

SADDLE

CLIFF

EVEN SLOPE

CONVEX SLOPE
(flattens out)

CONCAVE SLOPE
(gets steeper)

10.7 Route Profiles

Sometimes it is useful to get a rough idea of how the country would look if view from the side (its profile). A profile is best done at home or in base camp before following a set route or traverse. To make a profile:

1. place a straight edge of a piece of paper on the map along which the profile is needed;
2. mark off where the contour lines cut the paper onto the edge of the paper, noting the heights;
3. Prepare a vertical scale and a horizontal length forming a type of graph axes. The vertical scale will usually be smaller than the horizontal scale e.g. 1 cm = 100 metres vertical and 1 cm = 1000 m, otherwise the horizontal axis will be incredibly long and even steep terrain will be shown as relatively flat. These scales sometimes are shown on the map, otherwise use the horizontal scale given on the map (linear scale) and select an appropriate vertical scale for the differences in height to be travelled so that the profile will be of good proportions and will fit on a sheet of paper.) Using different scales for vertical and horizontal distances will, however give a **vertical exaggeration (V.E.).** In the example above, the vertical height has been exaggerated by and possibly make the slopes look steeper than what they really are. The VE is given by the vertical scale divided by the horizontal scale. In the example above,

$$V.E. = 1/100 \text{ divided by } 1/1000$$
$$\text{i.e. } 1/100 \times 1000/1 \text{ (invert \& multiply)}$$
$$\text{Or } 1000/10 = \underline{VE \text{ of } 10}$$

If using paired aerial photos as a stereopair, the V.E.
will be very large.

4. plot the heights and the places where their contours lie
   on the horizontal track; and
5. trace the topography by joining the plots using
   common-sense curves:

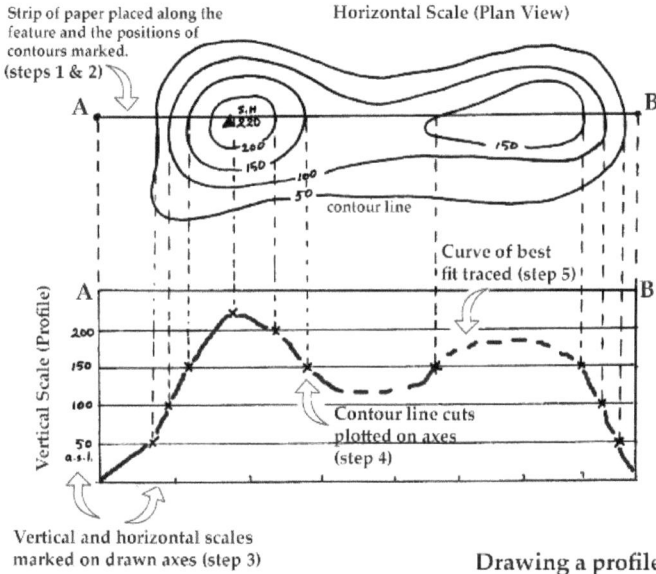

Drawing a profile

10.8 Gradients

The gradient of a slope is a measure of its steepness. Whilst it is convenient for space on a map and profile to use vertical exaggeration, they do not indicate the reality of the steepness of the ground to be walked.

The gradient of any slope is given by:

$$\text{Gradient} = \frac{\text{Difference in Height}}{\text{Horizontal Distance}}$$

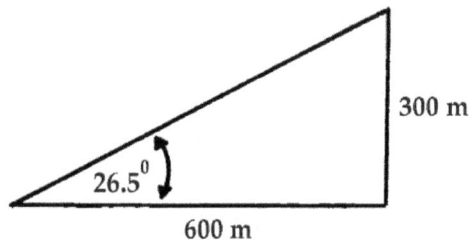

Gradient of 1:2

e.g.

1.5:1 gradient is 56 degrees

1:1	45 (extremely steep)
1:2	26.5
1:3	18 (steep hill)
1:4	14
1:5	11
and 1:20	3 (limit of easy cycling)

Calculate gradients (vertical rise/horizontal run) from the map or look side-on at the slope and use hand angles for an estimation of the gradient.

Walking uphill, one covers less distance horizontally because the paces are shorter. Walking down a gentle slope, the paces tend to become longer (only take very short paces going down steep hills!).

Gradient will greatly alter the estimation of distance travelled and thus the time of the trip. The time for walking over different gradients can be estimated from:
- **Naismith's Rule** - allow ONE hour for every 4 km. of distance measured on the map PLUS one hour for every 450 metres of actual climbing. e.g. consider the following trip:
  (Note: going downhill is taken as equal to a
  flat walking time. This is NOT true when the slope.is very steep).

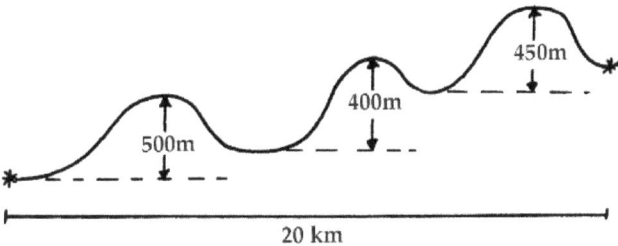

```
                     20 km
Map distanced walked = 20 km.        = 5 hours PLUS

Total vertical height = 1350 metres = 3 hours. so

            TOTAL TIME        = 8 hours.
```

- **Gradient Triangle** - the sides of the triangle give the actual distance walked up or down hill in 100 metres of distance as measured horizontally on the map e.g. up a 1:1 slope, a distance of 141 m is actually walked per 100 m of map distance:

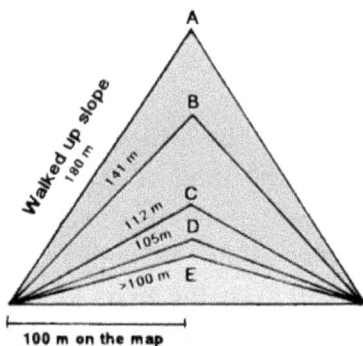

Gradient triangle

KEY	GRADIENT	DISTANCE		PACES			
				UPHILL		DOWNHILL	
		MAP	ACTUAL	Number/	length	Number/	length
		(METRES)		100m	cm.	100m	cm.
A	1.5 : 1	100	180	540	30	360	45
B	1 : 1	100	141	282	45	212	60
C	1 : 2	100	112	168	60	149	68
D	1 : 3	100	105	140	68	126	75
E	1 : 5	100	100	120	75	120	75

Chart of paces and gradients

NOTE: both of these methods assumes that:

- everyone is walking at a normal speed;
- paces are average (about 120 paces / 100 metres);
- visibility and weather is good; and
- the country is open or a track is being used.

Allowances have to be made for hindering factors such as vegetation, degree of fitness, injury, bad weather. An estimate of progress can be made by timing the party over a known distance from the map and in country typical of the route.

Vegetation is often a limiting factor or progress e.g.

OPEN COUNTRY/TRACK   4   km. in one hour,
OPEN RAINFOREST   1-2   km. in one hour,
DENSE RAINFOREST 0.5-1   km. in one hour,
TALL GRASS   0.5-1   km. in one hour,
BRACKEN FERNS   0.2-0.5 km. in one hour,
SWAMPS (varies) 0.1-0.2 km. in one hour.

10.9 Estimating Height
This can be done from:

- the map by looking at the heights (as shown by the contour lines) at the two places concerned (e.g. the base of the hill and its top) and subtract the lowest height from the uppermost one to give the relative heights between the two places. In very hilly country, the distances up and down slopes will have to be calculated because this will contribute greatly to the length and time of the trip.

- direct observation by knowing the horizontal distance between the top and the base of the high object (e.g. of the hill) and the angle that the top makes to the horizontal. This is done by:
    1. using the map to determine the straight-line distance from your position to the top of the hill;
    2. measuring the angle made from the horizontal to the top of the object (or base if looking down) using hand angles; and
    3. multiply the factor by the distance to the object (see 11.5):

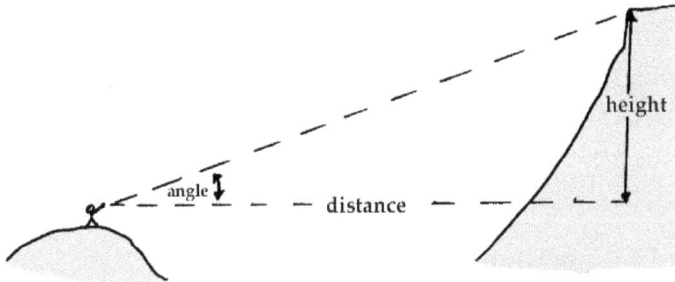

Estimating height

To estimate the height of a tall object such as cliff or tree, the base of which can be reached on foot, one simply paces out the distance from its base to a far spot so that the top can be seen and then use hand angles and the appropriate factor (see 10.5) to derive the height.

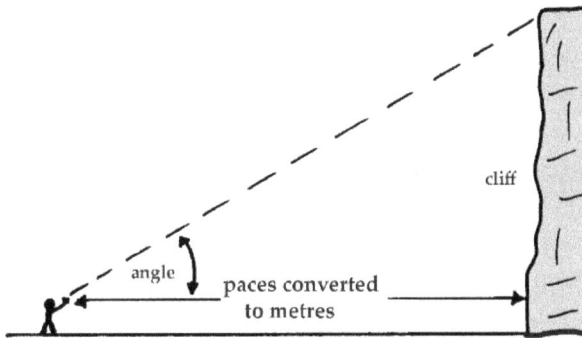

Find the height of a cliff or other tall object

For example: twenty paces out from a cliff, the top gives an angle of 77⁰. How high is it?

From tables (see 11.5) 77⁰ gives a factor of 4.3. Multiply this by the pace number (20) gives a height of about 86 paces or about 86 x (100/120) = about 70 metres.

10.10 Estimating Distance using Sound

Sound travels at about 330 metres per second at sea level and this value can be used to estimate distances such as:

- Distance to a far cliff using echoes.

  This is done by clapping the hands to make a loud echo. As soon as the echo is heard, clap again and continue clapping this way so that a clap is synchronized with an echo giving a rhythm. Count the number of claps in ten seconds. Divide this number by ten to give the time it takes for a TWO-WAY trip between the source of sound and the ear. Divide by two (i.e. one-way trip to the cliff) and multiply by 330 to give the distance in metres to the cliff.

- Distance from an approaching storm. This is useful to see whether or not threatening storm clouds are approaching or receding, especially at night. Wait until there is a flash of lightning and start counting in seconds (e.g."one...and... etc. equals one second). Multiply by 330 to get the number of metres then divide by 1000 to get it in kilometres. Do this several times to see which way the storm is travelling.

10.11 Lines on the Map
These include:

- LATITUDE and LONGITUDE are the most common internationally-used map coordinates are latitude and longitude. Latitude - runs across from left to right horizontally on the map as it is measured North or South from the Equator (zero degrees of latitude). Longitude - runs vertically up and down the map because it is measured east or west of the Prime Meridian (a line drawn through Greenwich near London).

The best way to remember this is that Longitude runs longways up the map and increases easterly OR westerly until 180^0.

Degrees of latitude and longitude are sub-divided into 60 minutes of arc and each minute into 60 seconds of arc. Some maps now also given these in decimals of a degree.

- GRID LINES are used for reference on each particular map. All maps are sub-divided into grids by vertical Eastings which increase in number as one moves further east and horizontal Northings as they increase going north.

These lines are not exactly parallel to latitude and longitude and will have different numbers on different scaled maps. They are useful for reference only on that particular map (or its series).

When giving **grid references**, always give the eastings (i.e. the numbers that go ACROSS the bottom or top of the map) first and then the NORTHINGS (i.e. numbers UP the sides of the map). **Grid squares** (bounded by two eastings and two northings) can be further sub-divided into 10 x 10 smaller squares to allow at least

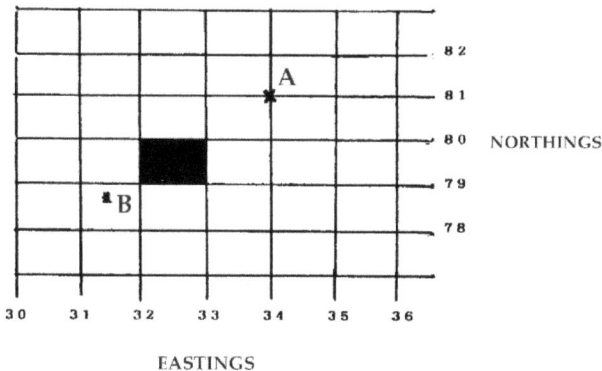

six-figure grid references e.g. Consider the following grid:

- the shaded area is grid square 3279;
- position A has a grid reference of 340810 (note that it is given as a six-figure reference to save confusion between the grid <u>square</u> of that number); and
- position B has a GRID REFERENCE of 315788.

If you need to be rescued, always give latitude and longitude as the other lines on the map (grid lines) may not have the same numbers of the maps of your rescuers.

10.12 Bearings on a Map

Bearings are directions to and directions from a position and can be given in many different ways with respect to a circular **compass rose** diagram e.g.

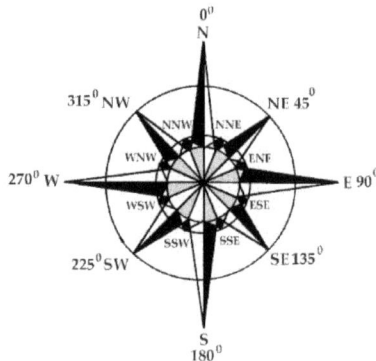

A Compass Rose

Thus, in the following diagram, to get to location B from location A, one would have to travel:

> **northwest or**
> **forty-five degrees north of west or**
> **west forty-five degrees north or**
> **map bearing of 315 degrees**

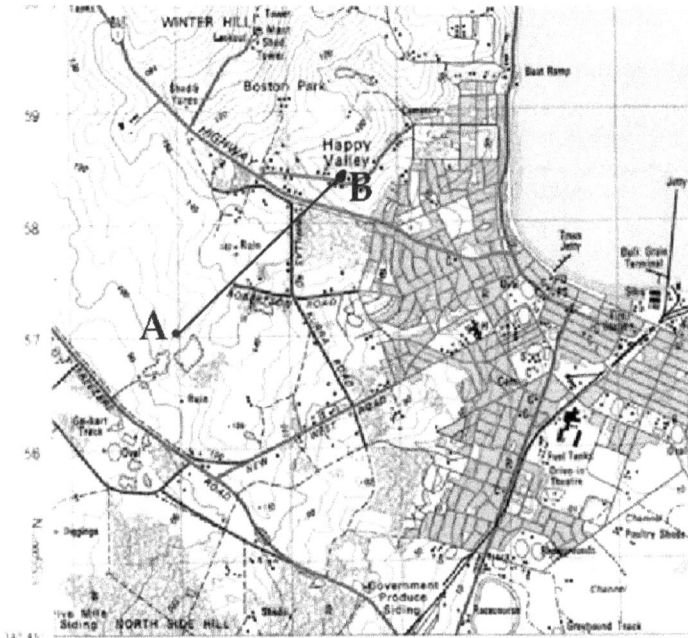

Of these identical directions, the less confusing is the **map bearing** (i.e. 315⁰) which is always taken <u>clockwise from north</u> (= zero degrees and 360⁰).

Remember: map bearings concern only directions on a

map and are different from compass bearings (see later)

Map bearings are taken from a position using a protractor. Whilst there are several types, the best is a 360^0 or circular protractor which has had a small hole (use a hot needle) made in its centre and a length (about 30 cm.) of fine, but strong string inserted through it and knotted at both ends. This string can be used to stretch out from the location (under the centre of the protractor) along the desired bearing in a straight line:

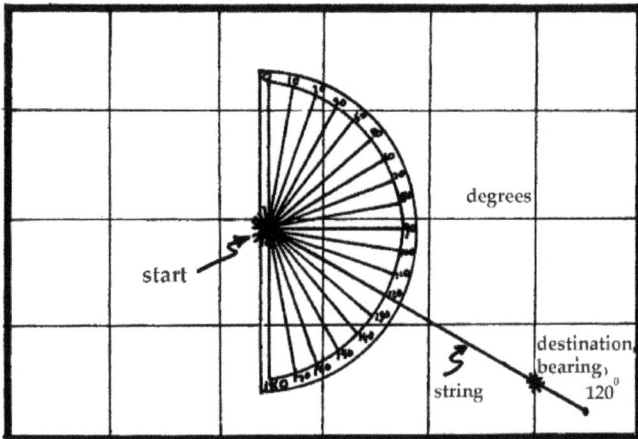

Using a Protractor on a Map

The string can also be used for measuring straight and curved distances on the map and, with a small stone on one end can be used as a simple vertical-angle measuring device (inclinometer).

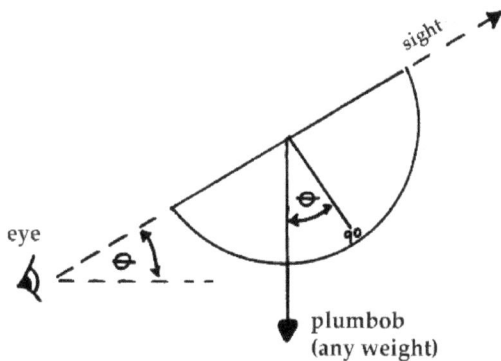

The protractor as an inclinometer

Estimations of angles can also be done by the methods of halves e.g. it is easy to draw a right angle of 90^0. Estimate halfway and draw a 45^0 line. Halve this for 22.5^0 and so on.

10.13 The Magnetic Compass

The Earth has a weak magnetic field due to moving currents in its liquid nickel-iron core and due to electrical currents in its surface crust. A suspended or floating magnetized piece of soft steel will follow the direction of the Earth's magnetic field. This direction is not exactly towards the Earth's North Geographic Pole (i.e. the top of the axis around which the Earth rotates) but lies towards the Earth's North Magnetic Pole which wanders about from year to year (it has been in northern Canada for some time). This is why Grid North from the map is <u>not</u> exactly the same as Magnetic North of the compass. The

Magnetic Declination is shown for a map's locality is shown at the bottom of the map for the year it was made. The current declination must be calculated by multiplying the declination/year by the number of years since the map was made.

Compasses are not accurate if:
- they are held near iron or iron alloy (e.g. wire fences, steel gates, rifles etc.);
- they are used near electricity (e.g. radios; telephone lines, electrical power lines, mobile phones, electronic tablets, laptops etc.);
- there are considerable iron deposits in the local rock, soil or termite mound (seen as hard, red-brown deposits which may be very extensive);
- they are near another magnet (e.g. another compass, magnetized knife etc.);
- they have been dropped or heated.

The best compasses are those which have:
- fluid to damp (settle) the vibration of the magnetic needle;
- good, clear numbers has provision for setting a bearing by rotating a bezel; and
- has luminous markings for following at night.

It should also have a strong lanyard so that it can be hung around the neck.

THE PRISMATIC COMPASS - having a prism or lens allowing for sighting upon an object:

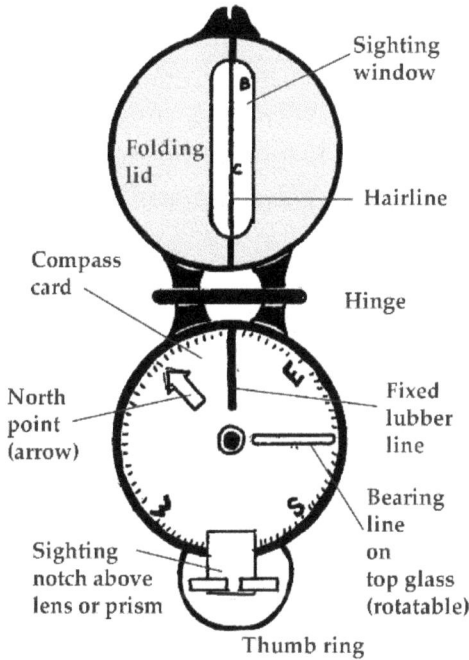

Sighting window

Folding lid

Hairline

Compass card

Hinge

North point (arrow)

Fixed lubber line

Bearing line on top glass (rotatable)

Sighting notch above lens or prism

Thumb ring

Parts of a Prismatic Compass

With the compass stretched open (i.e. flat, as shown above), the lid (and lubber line) is faced in the direction required and the bearing is read where the lubber line covers the outside rim of the card (e.g. about 045^0 magnetic in the diagram above...note that <u>three numbers</u> are given and the word magnetic is used so that there is no confusion with map bearings).

If a particular bearing is to be followed (especially at night):

1. orientate the compass so that the north point
2. is underneath the fixed lubber line;
3. rotate the top glass face until the luminous bearing line is above the opposite direction (i.e. your bearing + or - 180⁰) to your bearing. e.g. if you wish to go East, set 270⁰ (i.e. West) below the bearing line - check that this is right by facing the compass in the direction you wish to go - the bearing line should now be over the north point arrow;
4. follow the lubber line (lid first), keeping the bearing line over the top of the north point arrow.

If a bearing (or sight) is to be made on a distant object:

1. fold the lid so that it is now at right-angles to the rest of the compass;
2. fold the prism or the lens up so that the when the eye is place to it (and looking across the flat glass face of the compass), the numbers on the card can be seen (check that they are the correct numbers by having the compass face north ..see zero or 360 degrees);
3. place the thumb through the Thumb Ring and sight on the object by looking through the (now) vertical window. The centre of the hairline should be on the object;
4. holding the compass steady and horizontal, quickly glance down through the prism/lens and take the reading:

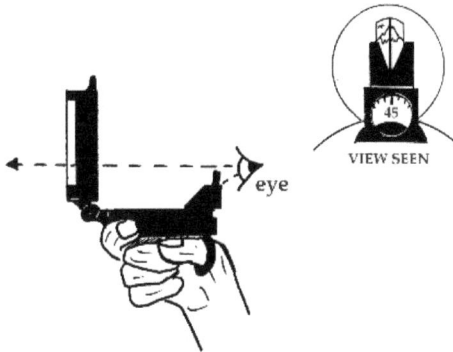

VIEW SEEN

Taking A Bearing

Note: These compasses are used by many of the world's armies for use with metric unit maps when great accuracy is needed - especially in jungle. The compass card is often marked-off in mils as well as degrees.

A mil is the angle subtended by one metre and one thousand metres (i.e. a kilometre).

1 metre

1 mil

1000 metres

There are 6400 Mils in one circle (i.e. 360^0).

ORIENTEERING COMPASS

This is a popular, flat plastic compass of reasonable accuracy which can also be used as a protractor:

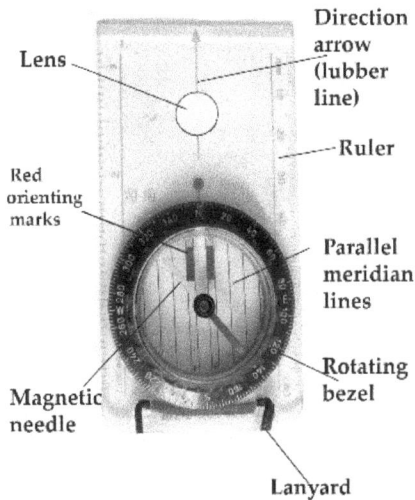

The Orienteering Compass

To set a course from a map:

1. place the compass on the map with one edge of the plastic base touching <u>both</u> the starting point and the destination (i.e. the fixed arrow – lubber line should be in the direction of travel);
2. turn the bezel until the red orienting marks of the bezel and the meridian lines (inside the bezel) lie parallel to the grid lines on the map;
3. the bearing required is read off from the top of the bezel (but use common sense to ensure that this would actually be the direction and not a bearing in the reverse direction!);
4. since the grid lines do <u>not</u> point to magnetic north, the

Magnetic Declination (also called Magnetic Variation) must be found for the location (discussed later) by calculating the declination for the current year and then adding or subtracting it by moving the bezel to the left (for subtraction) or to the right (for addition). This is the magnetic bearing (i.e. the compass direction) which is to be followed;

5. now rotate the compass so that the red part of the magnetic needle lies between the two orienting marks. Now follow the lubber line to get to your destination.

To orientate the map so that one can see what the country should be really like in the right direction from your position:

1. place the compass on the map with the lubber and meridian lines parallel to the Eastings (i.e. up-down lines) – the red part of the magnetic needle will be pointing North;
2. subtract or add the magnetic declination (depending on the locality) by rotating the bezel by that angle; and
3. holding the compass firmly on the map, rotate the entire map (and the compass on top) until the moveable red magnetic needle matches up to the red orienting marks on the bezel.

The map is now pointing in the right direction with respect to the ground and nearby land-marks should be able to be seen.

To take a magnetic bearing to a distant object:
1. hold the compass horizontal and still with the direction arrow (lubber line) towards the object;
2. rotate the bezel until the red orienting marks match up with (is below exactly) the moveable red magnetic needle;
3. read off the bearing from the bezel marks at the lubber line at the front.

10.14 Magnetic Declination

Magnetic declination (also called magnetic variation), is the angle on the horizontal plane between magnetic north (the direction the north end of a magnetized compass needle points, corresponding to the direction of the Earth's magnetic field lines) and true north (the direction along a meridian towards the geographic North Pole at the top of the axis of the Earth.

Now survey maps taken into the field will have grid lines – easting which are vertical and northings which are horizontal. However, in drawing these grid lines on the map, they may not correspond exactly with the actual parallels of meridians of the entire Earth. The slight difference in angle between the directions of the grid lines (e.g. eastings) on a map and those of the entire Earth which run from pole to pole is called the **Grid Convergence**. In most practical situations, such as hiking a local area covered by a local survey map, this convergence can be very small and sometimes can be ignored.

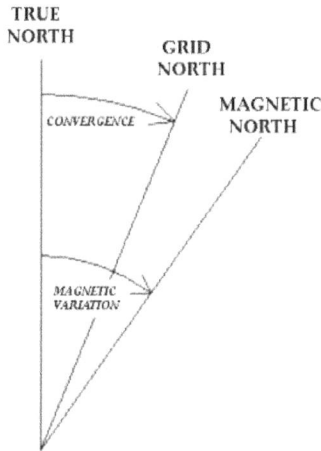

Magnetic deviation and convergence

The relative positions for Grid North and True North will change depending on the specific map used.

The values for magnetic declination for the survey map being used will be found at the bottom of the map. This will give the date at which the value was taken and the change in magnetic declination per year. The current declination must then be calculated from this change and the difference in years from then to now e.g. for Brisbane in eastern Australia, the declination from a 1975 map was 10 degrees, 35 minutes (10.58^0).

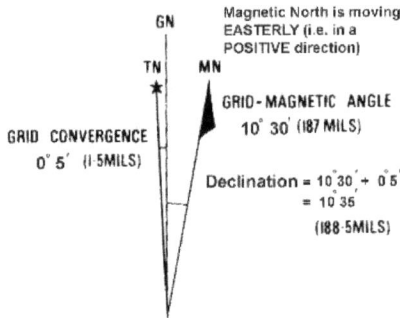

Magnetic North is moving
EASTERLY (i.e. in a
POSITIVE direction)

GN

TN   MN

GRID-MAGNETIC ANGLE
10° 30' (187 MILS)

GRID CONVERGENCE
0° 5' (1·5MILS)

Declination = 10°30' + 0°5'
= 10°35'
(188·5MILS)

Magnetic north is correct for 1975 and
moves easterly by 0.1 degree (2 mils) in
about three years.

**Magnetic declination diagram for
a map near Brisbane, Australia 1975**

For the year 2020, i.e. 45 years after the printing of this map, the declination for this locality would be:

$$10.5^0 + (45 \times 0.1^0/3)$$

(as the field changes 0.1^0 every three years)

10.5 + 1.5 = 12.0 degrees declination for 2020

Declination for other places for 2020 can be found at:
https://www.magnetic-declination.com/countries.php

It would be a good idea to find the declination for any proposed trip using this website from home before the trip.

The following map shows the major declinations for 2015 (from NOAA):

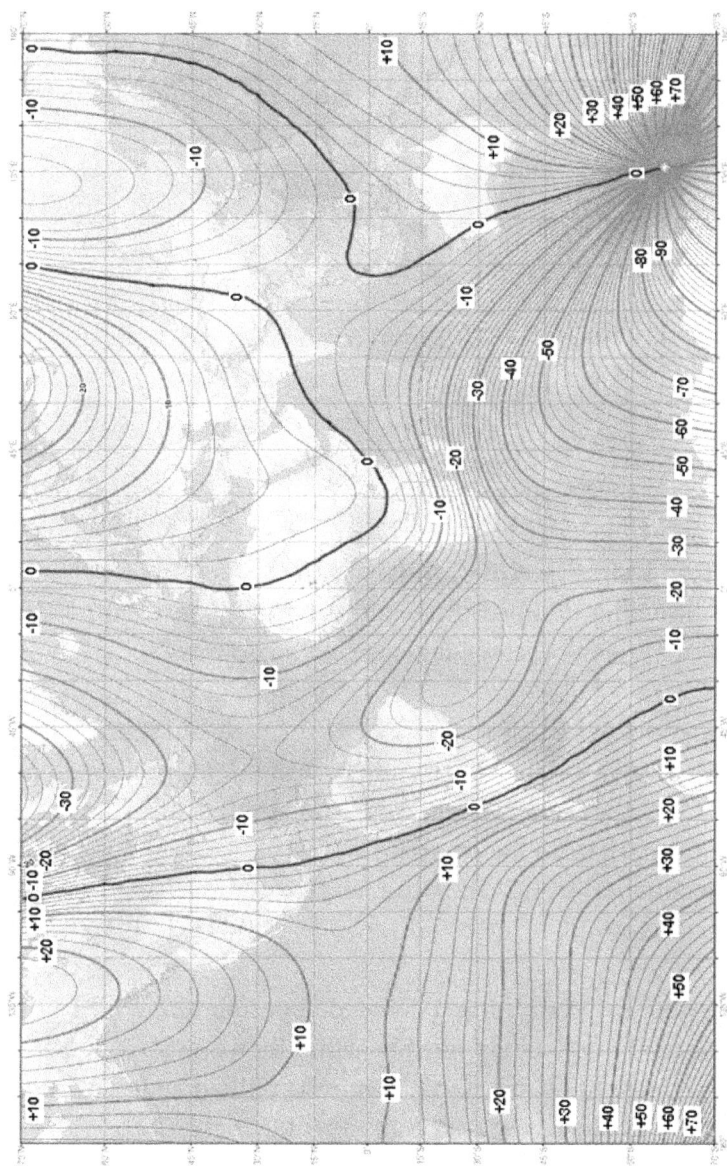

Remember that this data is for 2015 and so needs correction. It is given here as a rough guide to a locality's declination. A more recent map can be found at the NOAA site:

https://maps.ngdc.noaa.gov/viewers/historical_declination/

Current declination for map

_____

is _____degrees   (west or east?)

10.15 Using Declination with Maps

Remember that bearings on the map will not be the same as magnetic bearings taken using a compass.

For an EASTERY (or POSITIVE) declination when plotting a course onto a map FROM a compass, one ADDS the declination e.g. if the sighted direction to a landmark from the compass is 090^0 (i.e. east) and the local declination is $+12^0$ then the bearing to be marked on the map is (090 + 12) 102^0 Grid.

If one is determining a compass bearing along which to march FROM a map (grid bearing) then one SUBTRACTS the declination e.g. if the direction on the map is 270^0 then one will have to set the compass at (270-12) 258^0.

Remember for easterly (**positive**) declination:

+MGA
(for 'magnetic to grid, <u>add</u>')

If using a map in an area where the declination is WESTERLY or NEGATIVE (i.e. western Australia, south and western Africa, South America except Chile, eastern USA and Canada and the UK), the use the REVERSE action e.g. going from magnetic to grid, subtract.

10.16 Back Bearings and Resections

It is sometimes important to find the bearing in a reversed direction e.g. from a distant landmark to your present location or simply to reverse one's route.

 A back bearing can be found by turning about (i.e. at 180 degrees) and measuring the new bearing, or by adding 180^0 if present bearing is less than 180 or subtracting 180 if present bearing is more than 180. e.g. if the current bearing is 068^0 then the back bearing is $068 + 180 = 248^0$. If the current bearing is 250^0 then the back bearing is $250 - 180 = 070^0$.

A **resection** is used when the present position is to be found by obtaining at least three back bearings from easily seen distant landmarks well-spaced (hopefully around in a circle from your position) and then plotting these onto the map. This is done by:

1. taking three bearings on three separate landmark which must be:
    - easily seen from your position;

- recognized on the map;
- at some distance from you; and
- widely spaced around 360^0;

2. calculate back bearings from these bearings;
3. for each in turn, draw straight lines (traces) from these landmarks back along the back bearings;
4. where these lines cross will be your approximate present location.

If there is an error in your method (e.g. poor bearings, poor maths in calculating, thick pencil and poor use of protractor), the lines will pass through each other and form a **triangle of error**. The centre of this triangle should be your position. Check with local surroundings to see if they agree with your map position:

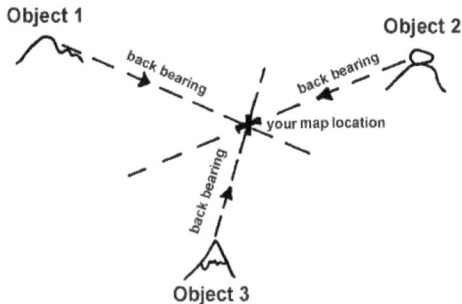

Taking a resection

Back bearings and resections should be taken occasionally as visibility permits to check your position en route - especially in rugged or timbered country or offshore.

10.17 Avoiding Obstacles

Travelling along straight-line routes (traverses) is not always possible because of natural and other obstacles (e.g. mountain, swamp, private property etc.). Avoiding and maintaining the normal route can be done by:

using right angles or simply stepping-around by sighting a distant (target) object on your line of route and beyond the obstacle and then:

1. taking three right-angular turns by setting the compass 90^0 to say the right;
2. waking an appropriate distance to avoid the obstacle;
3. getting back onto the original bearing by another 90^0 say to the left;
4. walking another appropriate distance around the obstacle;
5. taking another 90^0 turn say to the left;
6. walking the same distance as that first taken (in 2 above); then
7. taking another 90^0 turn say to the right to get back onto the original route.

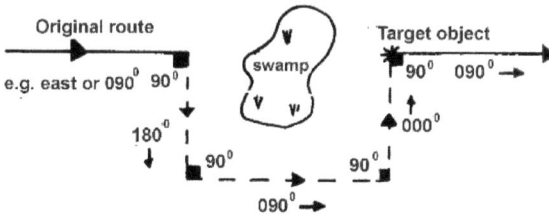

Original route   swamp   Target object

e.g. east or 090^0 90^0 90^0 090^0 →

180^0 000^0

90^0 090^0 → 90^0

Avoiding an obstacle

188

Using A Triangular Track by:

1. selecting a prominent land mark on the route on the other side of the obstacle;
2. sighting another prominent landmark off to the side;
3. walking to it; and then back to the landmark targeted on the side opposite your original position.

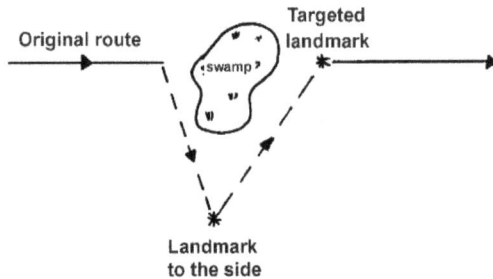

Avoiding an obstacle(2)

10.18 General Guidelines for Hiking

When planning the route or on the move consider:

- direct routes may not be practical - follow the county (e.g. walk around steep hills not over the top);
- ask permission of property owners - leave all gates, stock, crops and fences as found and do not wash in stock troughs;
- if blazing a trail, do so naturally without permanent damage nor pollution (e.g. place a piece of dead tree onto a stump of lower branch at eye-level; leave a cairn or arrow of stones etc.);
- follow man-made or animal tracks if possible;
- if off the track, follow ridges or creeks;

- small creeks may be overgrown so follow ridges in closely-vegetated country;
- when rock-hopping in creeks, take care - twisted ankles are likely;
- rivers and creeks may bend (meander) considerably, making the route much longer;
- try to maintain height - follow ridges or go around the hillsides. Up/down walking can be very difficult;
- plan on frequent rests in difficult country with a planned campsite being reached at least <u>two hours</u> before dark;
- keep a note of distance by counting paces (have several or all of the party doing this) - place a stone in a pocket for every 100 paces walked;
- keep in mind that most people <u>under estimate</u> distance walked. Only experience and good planning will improve the accuracy of your estimation of time and distance.

10.19 The Navigation Data Sheet

It is a good idea to prepare a sheet of bearings, routes etc. as a navigation data sheet well before the trip. These give details to follow and several of the party and the safety people at base should have a copy.

For each leg of the trip, show:
DATE: actual date or number of day (e.g. DAY 1 etc.);
DESTINATION DESCRIPTION i.e. a brief description of destination (e.g. Mike's Peak; creek crossing at; knoll at; etc.)

STARTING POINT for the first day should be noted at the top of the sheet and all subsequent starting points will be the destination of the previous day;

GRID REFERENCES: six-figure (at least) reference for each point or destination;

MAGNETIC BEARING: for setting the compass from the map (remember to subtract the variation from the map bearing for all places with easterly declination);

DISTANCE: usually in metres but it may be in paces;

TIME: in hours, allowing time to set up camps;

HEIGHT GAINED OR LOST: in general, the height up or down;

GOING: brief description of the land surface, vegetation, potential obstacles; landmarks etc. - any useful features;

E.T.D (Estimated Time of Departure) or start of each leg;

E.T.A (Estimated Time of Arrival) or end of each leg;

ESCAPE ROUTE: in case of accident, becoming lost or natural disasters (e.g. flood, fire etc.). This would have been generally planned before the trip from the overall route and so it may be applicable for several of the legs if they are part of the escape plan;

REMARKS: any applicable but brief comment (e.g. about possible camp sites; meeting or splitting the party; plants, animals, geology of interest; water available etc.).

Sample Navigation Data Sheets are given below. Copies should be enlarged and notes made in pencil (ink runs when wet) with the extra advantage of being re-useable:

NAVIGATION DATA SHEET

Day / /	From Grid Description	Grid	To Description	Grid	Distance	Magnetic Bearing	Going Terrain etc.	ETD	ETA	Escape Route	Comments

NAVIGATION DATA SHEET

Day / /	From Description	Grid	To Description	Grid	Distance	Magnetic Bearing	Going Terrain etc.	ETD	ETA	Escape Route	Comments

10.20 Direction by Natural Observation

It is always useful to be able to quickly check direction by means other than a compass. These are only rough guides but are useful for quickly checking bearings and if one does not have a compass:

10.20.1 By the Stars

The patterns of stars (constellations) also rise (generally) in the East and set in the West, taking a little less than 24 hours to do so – moving 15 degrees in one hour (another way of checking time to use hand angles and how far the sun or another star has moved):

POLARIS – THE NORTH STAR – in the Northern Hemisphere find the Big Dipper (also called The Plough) which is part of the constellation of Ursa Major (The Big Bear). Follow a line to a smaller version in Ursa Minor (The Little Bear) and look for Polaris, the bright star at the end of the handle. This is the North Star and is directly over the North geographic Pole. Drop a line straight down from this to the horizon gives North.

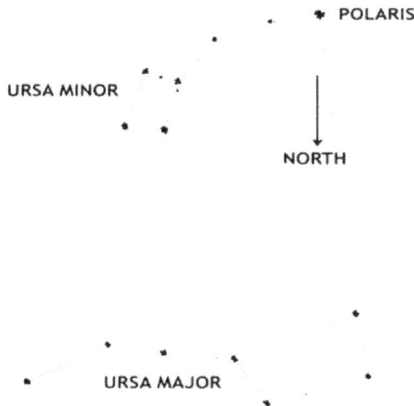

THE SOUTHERN CROSS – in the Southern Hemisphere, look low in the horizon in the southern part of the Milky Way (avoid the false crosses which are higher in the sky and are fainter). Locate the two pointers (including very bright Alpha Centauri) and imagine a line joining them. Take another imaginary line at exactly 90 degrees from the centre of the line between the pointers and extended it out to where it meets a line through the long axis of the Southern Cross. This will be the position of the South Celestial Pole which is directly over the South Geographic Pole. Drop a line down to the horizon and fix a landmark at this South position.

If the Pointers cannot be seen, but the Cross can, extend an imaginary line four-and-a-half lengths of the cross through its long axis. This will also reach the South Celestial Pole:

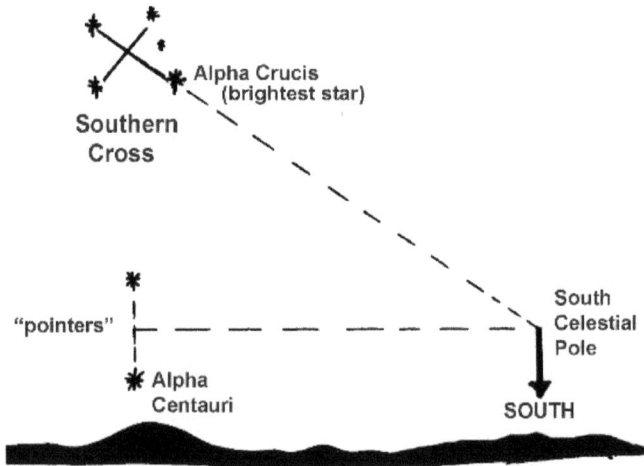

195

Note: in summer or in hilly or vegetated country, the low position of the Southern Cross may prevent it from being seen. The Southern Cross is best used in winter. When the Southern Cross is low or obscured, Orion can be used as it is higher in the sky.

ORION (the centre of which is often called the Saucepan) which is best seen in summer months (Nov.-May) in the southern hemisphere. It moves over the top or zenith of the sky and it is advisable to wait until it is directly overhead to use it to find direction (useful in hilly or vegetated country). Orion also can be seen in the southern sky in the northern hemisphere but it will appear upside down to the diagram shown below:

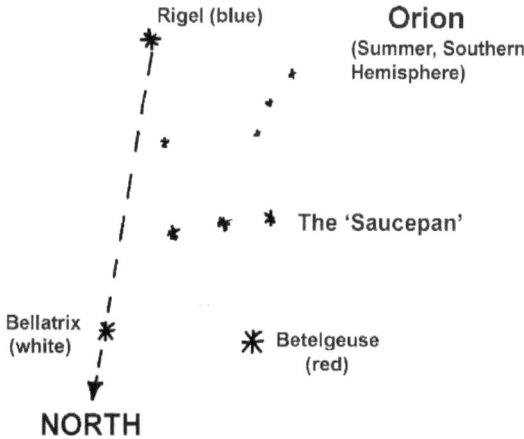

Rigel (blue)

Orion
(Summer, Southern Hemisphere)

The 'Saucepan'

Bellatrix (white)

Betelgeuse (red)

NORTH

A line joining Bellatrix (to the left of Betelgeuse) and Rigel (a very bright, blue-white star on the other side of the belt of Orion) runs roughly north (nearest Bellatrix) to south.

GEMINI and the star Procyon are found by finding Orion and then following a line from Rigel to Betelgeuse. Continue through to the two bright (white) stars close together. These are the stars of Castor (left) and Pollux (right) in the constellation of Gemini (the Twins). Immediately to the right of Betelgeuse is another bright star, Procyon.

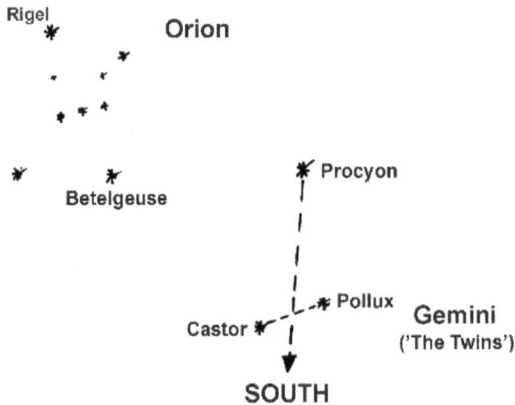

A line extended from Procyon to exactly between the Twins points approximately south. This should be used when the stars are almost overhead. Note that this diagram will be inverted in the northern hemisphere.

10.20.2 By the Moon
The Moon reflects light from the Sun well after (or before)

it has set (or risen). It takes 28 days for the Moon to orbit the Earth and go through its many phases. It can be used as a directional aid if it is <u>not</u> very high in the sky and if it is in an early or late phase as a crescent.

A line drawn through the outside curve of a crescent Moon which is low in the sky will point roughly towards where the Sun has set (West) or is about to rise (East):

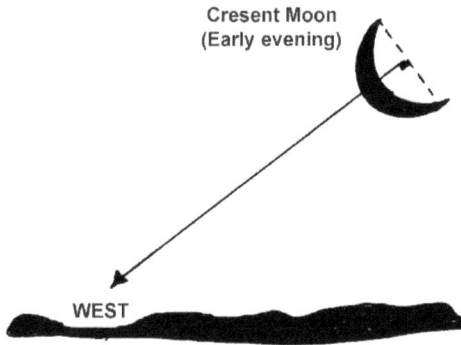

Another method when the Moon is higher in the sky, is to run a line from both horns of the crescent to the horizon. In the northern hemisphere, this will roughly point south and in the southern hemisphere this will be north.

10.20.3 Using the Sun

This works well in more southerly latitudes and better near mid-autumn and mid-spring in the southern hemisphere i.e. the periods of the equinox when the Sun is overhead at the Equator. It is also more accurate closer to noon. Remember that the Sun will rise in the east and set in the west only at the Equator. In other places it will be a little off the target at other times.

ANALOGUE WATCH METHOD - holding a watch horizontal, point the number 12 towards the sun and bisect the angle between this and the <u>hour</u> hand for the current time. This will give a rough approximation for north in the southern hemisphere. In the northern hemisphere, point the hour hand towards the Sun and the bisection of the angle between this and the 12 digit will be south.

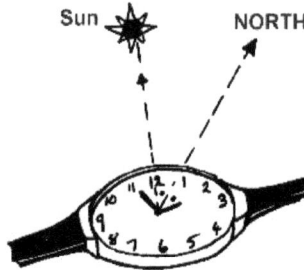

A SHADOW STICK may be useful to find direction using the Sun:
1. place a straight stick (about 1 metre long) vertically into the ground;
2. mark on the ground where the tip of the shadow lies;
3. wait about 15 minutes and mark the tip of the shadow again;
4. join both marks (where the tips of the shadow were). This line should approximately run east-west:

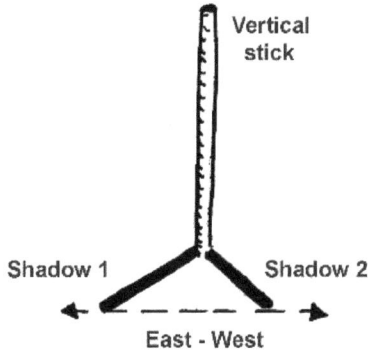

Vertical stick

Shadow 1   Shadow 2

East - West

Try to do this with a good field of view so that a prominent landmark can be seen for your preferred route to head towards.

A more accurate method (requiring the full day) is repeat this procedure for some time between forenoon and afternoon when the shadow will get to its shortest point. Mark off points at the end of the shadows during this time. The shortest shadow will point north-south and give the time as noon.

On a dull day, a shadow may (with luck) be found by holding a knife blade vertically on a reflective sheet of white paper and twirling it around. A faint shadow may be seen.

10.20.4 Using Other Natural Things
This requires good skill, observation and a lot of luck! The direction thus obtained will only be approximate and

useful only quickly check the approximate bearing of your compass or as a last resort if having no compass:

- in wet places having distinct seasons there may be more moss on one side of trees showing the direction receiving more Sun;
- in some countries such as northern Australia and southern Africa, termite mounds have their longer sides running along a north - south axis;
- ordinary ants may also build smaller mounds which are usually built facing the noon Sun; and
- prevailing winds may give an indication of direction and spiders will often build their webs on the lee side of trees away from the wind. Barchan or crescent sand dunes will also point in the direction of the prevailing winds with their crescents pointing towards the wind source. However, local terrain will change wind direction.

Chapter Eleven: Action if Lost

11.1 Prevention

The easiest solution is not to get lost in the first place! This is best achieved by:

- never go alone unless keeping to good tracks or if one knows the country well - even good bushmen get lost!
- Have a good idea where you are going with an action plan if lost e.g. head downstream, go in a set direction to a road or long ridge, or just stay put and shelter up etc.;
- be aware of your destination and the route, where you have come from especially if returning by this route. Regularly look back every few hundred metres and note landmarks - use sketches if needed. If in closed bush, leave landmarks such as piles of stones, mark on trees etc.;
- keep together - the party should go only as fast as the slowest member who should try to keep up but should always keep in view of another member;
- have good navigation skills and basic equipment (see chapter 11 navigation);
- have good personal equipment, especially emergency clothing for cold or wet weather;
- regularly compare maps with ground whenever prominent landmarks appear (care! - maps are not always right and the surface often changes, especially the man-made features printed on them!);
- when there is a good field of view (say about 200^0), check your position using back bearings (see Chapter

10 Navigation);

11.2 Immediate Action

<u>Immediately</u> you realize that you cannot recognise the route or present location:

1. STOP
2. KEEP CALM
3. CALL OUT (if you are last or first in a party)
4. WAIT and LISTEN
5. LOOK BEHIND and check where you have
6. come from. Move back a <u>short</u> distance on a trail and look for the trail or landmarks, otherwise -
7. STAY WHERE YOU ARE.

11.3 Major Plan

If this immediate action does not get results and some time of waiting passes then:

1. SIT DOWN
2. STAY CALM (have a drink or tea/coffee using small stove etc.)
3. CHECK MAPS, SKETCHES etc. if you have them and check location using back-bearings if any features are visible
4. WAIT and THINK for a little while
5. SIGNAL occasionally using three blasts on a whistle.

If there is no solution to the problem then discuss any

future action if you are in a group or think of the alternatives if alone.

There are now three alternatives:
1. **move to a recognized landmark** (hill, ridge, creek, tower etc.) which can be seen from your present position. Plan the route to it and leave a conspicuous note (who from, size & condition of party, time/date, destination) and a direction indicator (arrow of stones, sticks etc.); or
2. **move along the planned escape route** – which will be a simple turn and movement towards an obvious natural or man-made <u>linear</u> feature (e.g. stream, ridge, road, rail line power cables etc.).
Leave a note and direction indicators;
3. **stay put** - this is usually the best advice if you have <u>any doubts</u> as to your ability to move. <u>Do not attempt</u> to move with darkness a few hours away, in rain, snow, fog etc., in extreme heat or if there is an injury or an emergency unless one is forced to move away from flooding, fire or wind.

11.4 Waiting for Rescue (See Chapter 12: Communication and Rescue)
Once it has been decided to stay put (usually the BEST option) then a good camp site with shelter should be found. This should be:
- nearby or able to be found (notes/direction arrow) from your present position;
- close to a clearing (or place which could be easily

cleared) or bare hilltop or river flat so that a direction indicator (e.g. weighted orange ground sheets or panels in the shape of an arrow pointing to camp);

- near a source of water if possible;
- sheltered from rain, wind and sun; and be
- visible (e.g. smoky fire, cleared area; spread-out ground sheet or panels, large red cloth on pole in snow).

The camp should be well-established before dark otherwise do the best and make a quick shelter using natural features such as a large fallen tree, rock cave etc. and plan to wait. If you have the time or as soon as possible, this will mean:

- checking the immediate area for danger e.g. flood, potentially falling rocks, animal nests etc.;
- preparing shelter - if without a tent, build a native shelter (see Chapter 8: Shelter). If no shelter, use dry grass stuffed into outer clothing for warmth and sleep in a huddled position with arms and legs tucked in;
- making a camp fire - with some green bushes handy for making smoke during the day. Gather extra wood for night;
- checking food and water supplies with a view to rationing both as required – especially water if it cannot be easily replenished;
- make preparations for rescue such as packing up all gear, listen for sounds of rescue (have a roster if in a group); and then
- relax and try to keep calm and comfortable.

Searching the <u>immediate</u> area (do NOT wander far) for possible potential sources of wild food may be an option after a few days but any wild foods should be tested cautiously immediately and not when finally starving!

If you have left your plans with others, there should be a rescue within a short time after you have been missed. Keep occupied - practice bush craft skills such as building a shelter, clearing the immediate area of small bushes, play games (if children present) and tending any injuries.

Chapter Twelve: Communications and Rescue

12.1 In General

Communication is signaling between two persons or groups for the purpose of conveying a message.

When moving in large parties, the members of the group should be able to see those in front and behind, so communications should be simple hand or verbal signals. This is especially important in thick vegetation, at night or in bad weather.

Each member of the party (except the last) should check the well-being of the person behind and stop the group if anyone is slow, too far away or not seen.

The leader should ensure that the pace is not too fast for slower members.

All communications MUST be simple and clear. For these reasons, some simple rules should be followed:
- all detailed messages should be written down (before sending and as received);
- signals should never be made in jest;
- only ONE person for each group (i.e. SENDER or RECEIVER) should make the signals;
- after making a signal, the sender should wait a reasonable time for the receiver to comprehend or

decode the signal;

- simple, correct language or simple codes should only be used - complicated signals are confusing.
- Difficult words, numbers and grid references should be given twice and may be individually spelt out using standard letters or number pronunciations (see later);
- Send long messages in small amounts with acknowledgements between each part;
- never use slang or movie expressions unless understood by all;
- never use crude language; and
- never interrupt another party's communications unless absolutely important.

12.2 Emergency Signals

These signals should ONLY be sent in GENUINE cases of emergency:

12.2.1 S.O.S. (Save our Souls) morse:

$$\cdot \cdot \cdot \quad \_ \_ \_ \quad \cdot \cdot \cdot$$
"dit dit dit/ dah dah dah/ dit dit dit"

(NOTE: "dah" is THREE TIMES the time duration as a "dit" and the space or time between each element is the same as the duration of a "dit".)

This signal may be given with any SOUND device (e.g. whistle, horn etc.) or by any VISIBLE means (e.g. torch, mirror, markings on sand or snow, or using piles of stones or marking panels.)

12.2.2. Mayday (French: m'aidez = help me) Useful only as a verbal signal e.g. over a radio. This is usually repeated three times:

"mayday-mayday-mayday"
Followed by the message e.g. "This is…"

13.2.3. Pan is used if there is a concern about safety which requires timely but not immediate assistance. Given twice:
"pan-pan"
Followed by the message e.g. "This is…"

12.2.4 Any Signal Repeated in Threes: such as:
- three fires in a row e.g. three smoky fires in (grass/green leaves) for forest and grasslands but take care they are contained.
- black smoke (from rubber or oil) is best for sea, snow or desert;
- three blasts on a whistle repeated with a gap in between;
- three gunshots repeated; or
- any other signal in threes.

12.2.5 Red Flare at night or a smoke flare during the day. Especially useful at sea;

12.2.6 General Signal of a Frantic Nature e.g.

- wave a brightly-coloured cloth on the end of a long pole in a figure-of-eight pattern;
- rapid flashing of torch or mirror; or
- general noise such as a shout.

Once attention has been gained, more detailed signals can be given.

12.3 The International Morse Code

A	. _	dit dah
B	_ . . .	dah dit dit dit
C	_ . _ .	dah dit dah dit
D	_ . .	dah dit dit
E	.	dit
F	. . _ .	dit dit dah dit
G	_ _ .	dah dah dit
H	. . . .	dit dit dit dit
I	. .	dit dit
J	. _ _ _	dit dah dah dah
K	_ . _	dah dit dah
L	. _ . .	dit dah dit dit
M	_ _	dah dah
N	_ .	dah dit
O	_ _ _	dah dah dah
P	. _ _ .	dit dah dah dit
Q	_ _ . _	dah dah dit dah
R	. _ .	dit dah dit
S	. . .	dit dit dit

T	_	dah
U	.._	dit dit dah
V	..._	dit dit dit dah
W	._ _	dit dah dah
X	_.._	dah dit dit dah
Y	_._ _	dah dit dah dah
Z	_ _..	dah dah dit dit

Remember:

- Dah is three times longer than dit;
- Gaps between elements IN a word are the same duration as a dit.
- Words are separated by longer pauses.

Numerals:

1 ._ _ _ _ dit dah dah dah dah	6 _.... dah dit dit dit dit
2 .._ _ dit dit dah dah dah	7 _ _... dah dah dit dit dit
3 ..._ _ dit dit dit dah dah	8 _ _ _.. dah dah dah dit dit
4 ..._ dit dit dit dit dah	9 _ _ _ _. dah dah dah dah dit
5 ..... dit dit dit dit dit	0 _ _ _ _ _ dah dah dah dah dah

Signal Codes – are standard message terms and are sent as ONE WORD e.g.

- **AAAAA** etc ._ dit dah (repeated)

"I have a message"
- **AAA** (at end of sentence)
  "more follows"
- **EEEEE** etc   .   dit (repeated)
  "error - start from last correct word"
- **AR**   . _ . _ . dit dah dit dah dit
  "end of message"
- **TTTTT** etc   _   dah (repeated)
  "I am receiving you"
- **IMI** etc .. _ _ dit dit dah dah(repeated)   "say again -
  I do not understand"
- **R**   . _ . dit dah dit   "message received"

Some Useful Words (/ indicates break):

S.O.S.	. . ./_ _ _/. . .
SEND	. . ./. /_ ./_ . .
HELP	. . . ./. /. _ . ./. _ _ .
DOCTOR	_ . ./_ _ _/. _ ./_ /_ _ _/. _ .
LOST	. _ . ./_ _ _/. . ./_
NEED	_ ./. /. /_ . .
WATER	. _ _/. _/_ /. /. _ .
FOOD	. . _ ./_ _ _/_ _/_ . .
COLD	_ . _ ./_ _ _/. _ . ./_ . .
WET	. _ _/. /_

Morse Using Flags

If the other party can be seen, tie a coloured cloth to a long pole and use it to make exaggerated figure-of-eight movements:

DIT......swing on your RIGHT

DAH....swing on your LEFT

12.4 Flares
In general, they mean:

>RED..........Help/S.O.S
>WHITE.....Message understood
>GREEN....Returning to base

Remember:
- Any flare will generally be investigated if unexpected;
- Care should be taken with flares – instructions on the label should be followed carefully;
- The base of flares will be hot so take care;
- Bury in sand or extinguish in water when finished to prevent fires.

12.5 Bush Signals
Direction of travel can be shown by:
- an arrow-head of stones or sticks;

- an arrow-head carved into a tree;

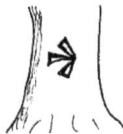

- cleft stick with long end pointing in the direction.

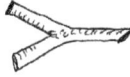

To indicate that a way should NOT be taken, block the path with a cross of sticks (upright) or stones (on the ground).

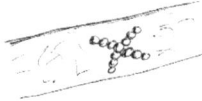

12.6 Ground to Air Signals

If involved in air search/rescue, the following codes are useful as they are known to pilots.

Rectangular panels (ideally 10m x 3m separated by at least 3m) are used. These may be made from several groundsheets weighted down with stones. A bright orange, light plastic sheet can be used as groundsheet, tent cover etc. and so is very useful and can replace such items in the back pack. Alternatively, vegetation, sticks, stones or coloured soil on a large bare patch of ground could be used.

The main signals are:

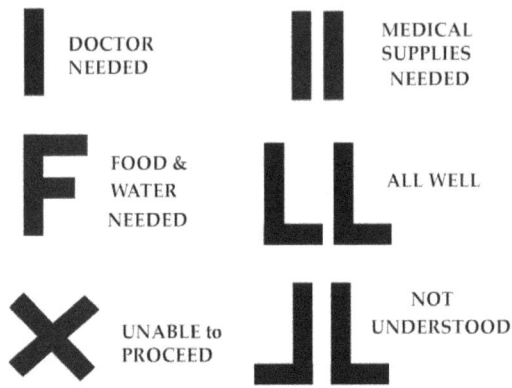

I DOCTOR NEEDED	**II** MEDICAL SUPPLIES NEEDED		
F FOOD & WATER NEEDED	**LL** ALL WELL		
X UNABLE to PROCEED	**⅃L** NOT UNDERSTOOD		

NEGATIVE (No)   AFFIRMATIVE (Yes)

N   **Y**

MOVING THIS WAY   INDICATE WHICH WAY TO PROCEED

→   **K**

NEED COMPASS

V   **□**

REQUIRE ASSISTANCE

12.7 Body Signals - Ground to Air

Note that some signals require the body to be SIDE-ON to the aircraft. A coloured cloth is to be held in the hand for the YES/NO signals, especially if a landing is being attempted:

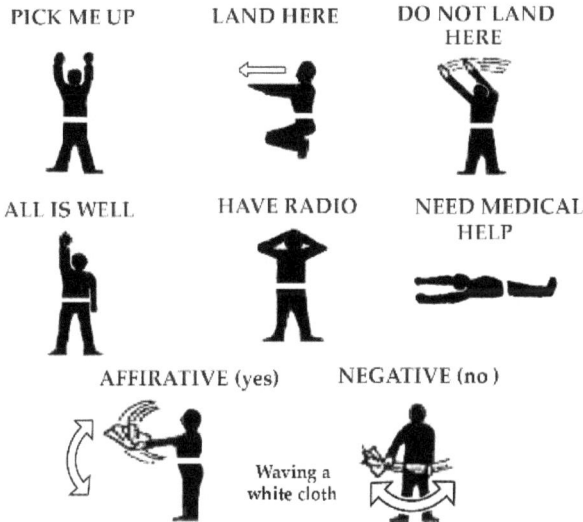

PICK ME UP	LAND HERE	DO NOT LAND HERE
ALL IS WELL	HAVE RADIO	NEED MEDICAL HELP
AFFIRATIVE (yes)	NEGATIVE (no)

Waving a white cloth

Aircraft replies:
- MESSAGE UNDERSTOOD: aircraft will rock its wings from side to side or show a green light at night;
- MESSAGE NOT UNDERSTOOD: aircraft will fly in a tight right-hand circle or show a red light at night.

12.8 Radio

Some hikers may take a small hand set or walkie-talkie but most will not. Most small sets have very limited range and are subject to interference by magnetic fields such as from powerlines. Know the rescue frequencies which could come in handing if search and rescue parties are nearby.

12.8.1 In general most people do not carry radios unless the field trip is of a difficult nature in extreme conditions or if there is to be an extended stay. In these cases, good radios of reasonable range are needed. They are usually larger and heavier than most popular handsets but have greater range and endurance.

For emergencies use Channel 16 VHF (2182 kHz) for marine distress and use Channel 88 (27.88 MHz) for 27 MHz hand-held receivers.

Mobile telephones are more practical IF they have coverage in the area (check beforehand!)

Radios should be treated carefully e.g. operated by one person who has some training, kept dry, free of dust and out of direct sunlight if not in a case and be carried in a pack with good supporting straps;

Small radios, walkie-talkies, usually operate only as line-of-sight devices, so major hills, especially if containing iron-rich rock or soil will stop radio waves.

For best transmission, always seek the highest point and reception is often better at night when the electrical disturbances of the atmosphere are less.

Small handsets are useful at close range (in forest and rescue cases when parties are near). Even if a small handset cannot send over a long distance, it may be able to receive transmissions from more powerful sets, giving some comfort to those being rescued or to help the party move towards directed safety.

Very rough radio direction-finding may be possible with a small pocket radio which often have a directional aerial (AM only). Usually these are coils of wire wrapped around a ferrite rod within the case. Using the AM tuner, a commercial radio station can be located and the radio rotated until the MAXIMUM signal is received. This will then be at **right-angles** to the transmitting station but will give a choice of two directions!

If a large-scale map (even an atlas will do) is at hand, the direction FROM this station can be roughly located by taking the most obvious direction to such a radio source e.g. in a large town of city.

If several local stations can be received from a variety of bearings then a more accurate location for one's position can be found. Again, this is best tried at night when signals are stronger.

12.8.2 The Phonetic Alphabet (letters)
When using a radio, always use CLEAR, CORRECT, radio terms when spelling out messages. Say: "I SPELL.." before giving the spelling and then make the pronunciation clearly.

The following alphabet codes are given with their formal

PHONETIC pronunciations (i.e. the way they should be sounded with emphasis in capitals):

A	ALPHA	AL fah
B	BRAVO	BRAH voh
C	CHARLIE	CHAR lee
D	DELTA	DELL tah
E	ECHO	ECK oh
F	FOXTROT	FOKS trot
G	GOLF	GOLF
H	HOTEL	hoh TELL
I	INDIA	IN dee ah
J	JULIET	JEW lee ett
K	KILO	KEY loh
L	LIMA	LEE mah
M	MIKE	MIKE
N	NOVEMBER	no VEM ber
O	OSCAR	OSS cah
P	PAPA	pah PAH
Q	QUEBEC	keh BEK
R	ROMEO	ROW me oh
S	SIERRA	see AIR rah
T	TANGO	TAN go
U	UNIFORM	YOU nee form
V	VICTOR	VIK tah
W	WHISKEY	WISS key
X	X-RAY	ECKS RAY
Y	YANKEE	YANG key
Z	ZULU	ZOO loo

12.8.3 The Phonetic Alphabet (NUMBERS)

Say "I spell figures...." and give the pronunciation:

0	ZERO	ZEE row
1	ONE	WUN
2	TWO	TOO
3	THREE	THUH ree
4	FOUR	FOW er
5	FIVE	FIFE
6	SIX	SIX
7	SEVEN	SEV en
8	EIGHT	AIT
9	NINE	NINE er
Decimal point	0.1	Day see mal
Full stop	.	FULL STOP
Comma	,	COMMA
Hyphen	-	HY PHEN

Before sending a message, write (using pencil) it out in full using any Morse code or phonetic symbols required. If the message has to be sent to a rescue party or given to another person, tear it out carefully from this book. Sample of blank message forms are given on the next page

MESSAGE FORM

DATE: _____ TIME:_____

FROM: _____

TO: _____

SUBJECT: _____

LOCATION:_____

_____

MESSAGE: _____

_____

_____

_____

_____

_____

_____

_____

ACTION TO BE TAKEN: _____

_____

_____

_____

_____

_____

_____

Signed_____

MESSAGE FORM

DATE: _____ TIME:_____

FROM: _____

TO: _____

SUBJECT: _____

LOCATION:_____

_____

MESSAGE: _____

_____

_____

_____

_____

_____

_____

_____

ACTION TO BE TAKEN: _____

_____

_____

_____

_____

_____

_____

Signed_____

12.9 Rescue

Search and rescue organizations are very efficient <u>once they know about the need</u>. Always leave trip details with a responsible person (police, ranger, club official, relative) and a time after which a search is required.

<u>Never</u> **request nor cause a rescue unless there is a real need** e.g. serious injury, threat of disaster (fire, flood etc.)

Remember:
- if one has left details, help WILL arrive;
- prepare good signals which are clear and brief;
- be prepared for rescue - there may not be time for much packing;
- keep up morale - keep self and others busy;
- keep a look-out at all times for the rescuers; and
- carry-out all instructions given by the rescuers.

12.10 Search Methods

Rescuers will follow definite procedures in attempting the rescue, such as:
- they will usually start from the last known point of contact (usually the starting point of the trip);
- they will generally follow the planned route (so leave directions when and where the route is varied);
- they will make assumptions about terrain (if difficult) and weather - assuming that the lost party will head for obvious places of shelter or potential rescue sites;
- having searched the obvious places, a wider search pattern will be started; and

- they will be looking carefully so make signals.

12.11 Helicopter Rescue

A most common rescue when the area to be searched is within helicopter range. The rescue may be carried out by landing (if suitable) or most likely by winching-out if the terrain or vegetation does not allow a landing.

Landing Rescue - this can only be done if there is a suitable landing site or if the winds are suitable. A landing site should be chosen so that there is:
- clear visibility;
- firm ground - compact snow, make a large raft of small logs on muddy ground;
- good wind direction - an obstruction-free approach and exit must be planned so that both are into the wind;
- wind direction indicated - use a smoky fire or large, colourful thin sheet on a pole; and
- plenty of cleared, level space around the site.

It is best to use a natural site, such as a bare hill or ridge, a sand bar or flat river bank on a stream or a wide, flat rock ledge.

If there is no obvious natural site nearby, then the most level, least vegetated place must be found and cleared to the ground to give a circle at least <u>26 metres</u> in diameter with further clearing to about 60 centimetres above ground to an <u>additional 15 metres</u>. The centre of this site should be marked with a large "H" and some form of wind indication (smoky fire or a "T" sign placed with the long arm pointing in the direction that the wind is going).

If in very high country (i.e. above 1830 metres = 5000 feet), helicopters find control difficult so try to move to a lower site to build the landing pad - a track should be made to the original camp if some members of the party cannot be moved).

After the helicopter has landed:
- only move when the pilot gives the signal (a wave, thumbs up or the support crew may come over) – otherwise stay in sight at the edge of the landing pad;
- never approach from the rear - it is a blind spot for the crew and there is a tail rotor which may swing around;
- never approach from downhill - the rotor blades will be hit. approach uphill or along a flat surface;
- approach from one position (if a group), moving from any point from the side to the front of the helicopter:
  - **keep low** - keep the body bent low, do not have packs on backs (carry or drag) and remove or secure any hat or item which will be blown away;
  - keep sharp objects (tent poles etc.) away from the sides of the helicopter and take care when inside;
  - follow all instructions carefully;
  - sit where directed - put gear where directed (it may be left behind!) - fasten seat belts as directed; and
  - do not unfasten belts nor leave the helicopter until

directed to do so.

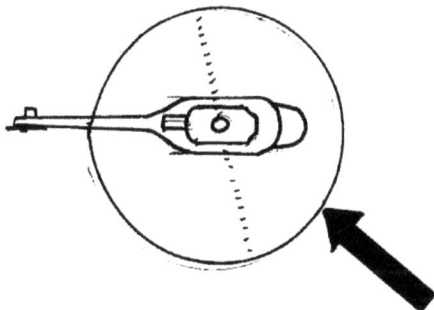

Approaching a helicopter on flat ground

Winch Rescue - from unsuitable land or from water. WARNING - helicopters may build up a lethal amount of static electricity when flying. Wait until the harness has touched the ground or water before touching it.

Using a double lift - in most cases a crewman will be winched down to support the person who is in a second harness:
1. once the harness has been tightened, keep the legs together and the arms straight down by the sides; and
2. the crewman will wrap his/her legs around the middle of the rescued person's waist and will support their head

A Double Lift

Using a single lift - the empty harness will be lowered to you:
1. after it has touched the ground, pick it up and place it over the head and under the armpits so that the supporting cable comes up from about mid chest; and
2. give the pilot a THUMBS UP SIGNAL and immediately move the arms back so that they are straight down the sides of the body.

A Single Lift

From both lifts, once you are level with the door you will be turned around and taken into the helicopter. <u>Do not undo the harness - follow all instructions.</u>

12.12 Carrying the Injured
Care must always be taken when carrying the injured.

Never attempt to move a person with a <u>suspected back injury</u> unless their life is in danger - then carefully slide a flat, rigid object (e.g. plank, strong raft of saplings stretcher etc.) underneath their body taking care not to jar the spinal column.

For other injuries, some of the more common carries are:
A SIMPLE STRETCHER - poke two long saplings inside and through the ends of a sleeping bag.

Alternatively, place the two saplings through the legs of a spare pair of long trousers or the arms of two long-sleeved shirts. Three belts (one at each end and one in the middle) looped around the saplings from side-to-side may strengthen the stretcher.

Another method is to place a blanket (not a slippery plastic groundsheet) on the ground, lay the two saplings onto the blanket in the required size of the stretcher and then fold the blanket over the top. The weight of the casualty should keep the blanket intact but safety pins or knots would help.

A variation of this is to lie the casualty on the centre of a blanket and roll up each side. Several people (say at least two) on each side can then lift up the blanket by grasping the side rolls.

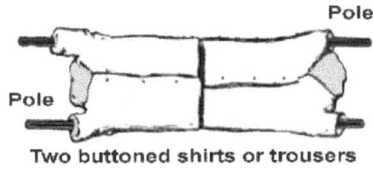

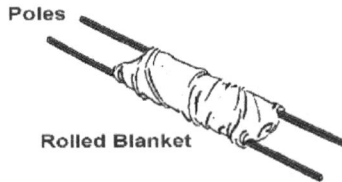

Improvised stretchers

Blanket carry

FIREMAN'S CARRY (conscious casualty) - ensure that any injury is well-padded and secure from movement. To prevent injury to self and casualty:

1. get the person to stand, kneel in front with the knees

bent (so that the legs will do the lifting, not the back which should be straight);

2. pass your arm straight between the casualty's legs so that it curls around and grips one leg at the knee;

3. with the other hand, grasp the casualty's wrist. Whilst pulling down on this arm, stand upright by slowly straightening the knees and pulling the casualty across your shoulders.

The Fireman's Carry

USING A SLING (unconscious casualty) - this method must only be used if there is no other help available. To make a sling carry:

1. make a strong, continuous loop (from several belts, rope, strips of knotted etc.) about a metre to one-and-one-half metres long;

2. lay it under the casualty's middle (the casualty is face

up) so that two ends of the loop protrude on either side of the casualty;

3. lie between the casualty's legs (face up) and reaching back, put your arms through the protruding ends of the loop, thus securing your body to that of the casualty;

4. grasp their left arm and roll over towards the right side until the casualty is on top; use your hands and knees to slowly rise to the standing position.

The Sling Carry

TWO PERSON SEATS - these are better if the casualty can use their arms to hold the carriers around their shoulders. The carriers can simply hold their arms or for a bigger person, their hands beneath the casualty's thighs. If the casualty has arm injuries, a two-handed seat is used so that the carriers can pass their other arms behind the casualty's back, gripping together or gripping the casualty's shirt:

Two-person Seat

DRAGGING – is not recommended across rough surfaces but could be used across snow using a waterproof and strong groundsheet or tent (folded) or across sand using a blanket.

For rough but flat surfaces free of obstructions such as bushes (e.g. grassy plains), a North American Travois may be constructed using lashed tent poles or any timber at hand. The casualty is laid along the Travois on whatever padding can be arranged.

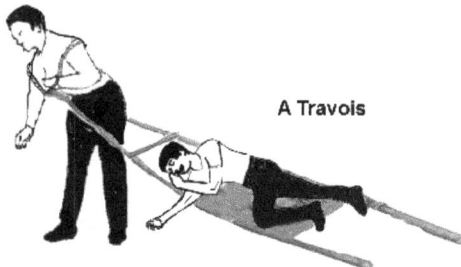

A Travois

Chapter Thirteen: Miscellaneous

13.1 Climbing Hints

During the normal walking trip there should <u>not</u> be the need for serious climbing.

13.1.1 Basics

A few basics are given below in case some climbing is needed in <u>emergency situations</u>. This includes:

- selecting the <u>right place</u> - carefully survey the area to be climbed and think about it before climbing. The direct route may not be the best. Look for easy places such as a wide crevice (up which one can chimney) with ledges for resting. Stand back and check that ledges do not slope forward (away from the face) and that their surface is not too smooth - the best footholds and ledges slope into the cliff;
- check the nature of the rock - badly fractured rock or very hard, smooth rock with rounded surfaces will be difficult;
- try to avoid scree slopes (long slopes of piled, fallen rock) and over-hanging snow cornices which may suddenly give way;
- if in a party, send the best climber first who can then rig a hand or safety line for the others. Do not rely upon trees (they may have shallow roots) or tree roots (they may be dry and brittle) as hand-holds;
- use safety lines whenever possible - a handline may be useful as an extra grip when climbing a difficult section. This should be firmly fixed to a good anchor

point (e.g. a solid rock pinnacle or at least a well-rooted, large tree) using a non-slip knot (see Chapter 9). If the climb is difficult or over about five metres, a safety line should be rigged;

Climbing a Chimney

- if climbing up - the best climber would have to go first without a line or if part-way up a slope, the climber may have a safety line attached; and
- whether going up from part way up a cliff or going down a cliff or slope, the climber should be tired to a safety line and belayed by a competent and strong person well-anchored using a tight bowline around the waist using a separate anchor rope. The belaying man passes the safety line through one hand, around the arm, back and the other arm and then plays it out (keeping tension) as the climber moves. should the climber slip, the belay man will tighten the grip and pull both arms into their chest.

The climber has the rope fastened around their chest above the diaphragm using a bowline and two half-hitches (see Chapter 8) with plenty of spare rope at the end of the knot (especially with nylon which tends to slip);

Belaying A Climber on a Safety Line

Climbing requires maximum friction and grip. The best boots have rubber soles and good ankle grips although some professional climbers prefer light-weight shoes with good soles. In mud, snow or on sharp-edged rocks such as limestones, special toothed-edged boots or attachments such as snow/ice crampons or rock tricounis may be needed. These are specialized items of equipment and normally would not be taken on a trek unless the conditions were anticipated.

13.1.2 Use of Footholds and Handholds
Climbing is a conscious effort. One must always be looking for the best solid footholds or handholds. The

climbing route is dictated by such searching. In climbing:

- the boot or at least a toe or heel of the boot should always be placed flat-on to the rock surface, digging the toes or heels into any available crevice.
- it is a good idea to have three points of contact (e.g. two feet/one hand or the backside/two feet etc.) when climbing, using different parts of the body alternatively.
- take short movements - do not reach too far nor stretch on tip-toes.
- use the leg muscles rather than arms i.e. push rather than pull;
- if the foothold or handholds looks uncertain, try wobbling it with the foot or hand before adding any weight;
- always take care in slopes which have fractured or loose surfaces as some holds may give way;
- also be wary of slots, cracks or holes which may contain spiders, snakes etc. and
- do not rely on grass tussocks for grip.

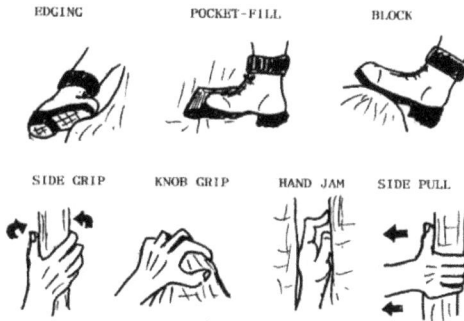

Some Climbing Grips

13.1.3 Abseiling

This is a quick and easy method of going down a rock face or very steep slope but requires confidence and control. There are a variety of devices which are used specifically for abseiling such as harnesses, rappel racks and descenders. If any trip requires a serious descent requiring a difficult abseil then one should seek training and learn how to use the specialized equipment and undergo some simple trials under supervision before any serious abseil is undertaken.

It may eventuate that the only way forward in an emergency situation is by abseiling down a slope or small cliff. In such a case, it would be hoped that part of the group supply would include at least 100 metres of good rope, preferably nylon climbing rope only used for that purpose. This can be easily plaited for carrying. For a simple classical abseil requiring only a length of rope the following steps are advised:

1. securely anchor the rope;
2. throw the free end of the rope over the cliff,
3. making sure that it reaches the bottom without snagging (a plaited rope thrown well falls better);
4. stand astride the rope, reach behind (with the hand most used) and lift up the down side of rope and pass it around the hip, across the chest and over the opposite shoulder;
5. gripping the rope firmly in the hands above and below the body (arms slightly out-stretched), take the tension on the anchor point;

6. lean backwards with the feet flat-on to the surface; and
7. keeping the legs at right-angles to the surface, slowly walk down the cliff (leave jumping to the experts), controlling the rate (SLOW) with the <u>hand behind</u> whilst the hand in front steadies the rope.

If there is a group and the rope is needed below, the last person can pass the rope around a tree thus doubling the strands of rope. This assumes that there is enough rope for both strands to reach the bottom. The last person then abseils down the double strand of rope but care is needed to grip BOTH strands together. Only for the experienced! Once at the bottom, the rope can be pulled down.

WARNING: Nylon rope is very slippery and will get hot if you go to fast. If a carabiner (metal ring with a snap lock) is used remember to completely close its lock and do not slide fast on nylon and then stop for a while as heat from friction on the carabiner may melt through the rope.

**Abseilling using a double rope
(lone or last descender)**

Instead of the harsh reality of the classic abseil, one can tie a good bowline of double strand rope around the waist and thread the climbing rope through a large carabiner looped into waist rope.

13.1.4 Using a Prusik Knot to Climb

The Prusik knot method of climbing up a single rope was briefly described in Chapter 9. This is a method of climbing is slow and requires skill and much energy. Three separate Prusik knots and their loops are made around the rope (see Chapter 9 for details of this knot). The other ends of each knot (i.e. the ends away from the rope to be climbed) are made into three separate loops or lengths depending upon body size, but generally about one metre.

The three Prusik knots and their loops are arranged so that there is:

- one free loop for EACH of the feet to act like stirrups so that the feet can freely move in or out; and
- one loop tied around the chest with a firm, non-slip bowline or even a sitting sling and bowline (the length on this loop may be shorter).

Try it for size standing at the foot of the rope, the feet should comfortably fit the loops with one leg straight and the other bent (the knot being higher up the rope). The knot attached to the chest loop should be above the level of the chest.

The single rope is then climbed by:

1. slipping the one Prusik knot which is not under tension (the other two are taking the weight) up the rope;
2. then put weight onto that loop and retain tension on one other knot;
3. reaching down and pull up the other knot which now has had the weight taken off it; continue this sequence of changing weight on two knots whilst pulling up the third knot which is free to move.

Climbing using a Prusik knot system

Whilst climbing, making sure that the Prusik knots are kept in a good, symmetrical shape (if they tangle, they won't move - rest on the other knots and untangle any damaged knot). Use any nearby wall for extra bracing.

13.2 Crossing Water
This should never be attempted during flood, and be very cautious at all other times.

Fast water has great strength and moveable rocks underfoot if shallow. Slow water usually is wider but can be deep.

Before crossing:
- ensure that all items of the pack are secure; choose a good, safe place where the water is narrow and shallow and hopefully with the bottom clearly visible;
- if the footing is good and flat with no visible sharp projections, then remove shoes and socks. Tuck the socks into the boots and hang them around the neck. On the other side, thoroughly dry the feet before replacing socks and boots. If boots must be worn at the crossing, remember to dry them thoroughly as soon as possible.

When crossing:
- use a walking stick or go in pairs if the water is only up to the knees;
- take care where the foot goes – testing the footing before weight is applied;
- for faster and deeper water, use a <u>rigid</u> support and cross in a group - a rope can be rigged and used as a safety line after the first group has crossed;
- if alone, cross sideways facing the stream flow and use a stout pole as a support to assist.

Stream flow

Wading a Stream

If the water is slow-flowing, deep and free from obstacles (and dangerous animals such as snakes, some fish and crocodiles etc.) then swimming may be required but do not attempt this in cold conditions with potential for hypothermia. If conditions are suitable:

1. strip off and wrap clothes and belongings in a large plastic bag and tie it securely or tightly seal the backpack (ensuring that it will float – if not, a raft may have to be built);
2. swim breaststroke with the pack in front. A useful life-preserver can be made by knotting the legs of long pants together and trapping the air in them by bringing the open end sharply down on the surface of the water. Hold the belt or rim of the trousers under the water to keep the air inside the legs. Float by lying slightly over the inflated legs whilst keeping the belt pulled down below the water;
3. on the other side, dry clothes and continue.

Trouser life-preserver

13.3 Country Code of Behaviour

When walking in the country remember that you are the intruder and that you should pass through it with minimum effect on natural and man-made objects.

Country people are usually very friendly and interested in visitors provided that they and their property are treated with respect.

Whether the area is a National Park or not, all natural things should be left alone and conserved as much as possible.

A general Country Code of Ethics would be:

- ask permission to enter private property, especially Indigenous Peoples' traditional lands (keep off sacred sites) obtain the appropriate permits to enter National Parks well in advance;
- leave everything as it was found, especially gates, huts, water tanks, tracks and the like;

- leave animals and plants alone if possible – only dead timber and some small saplings may have to be used;
- do not go near livestock nor bathe in stock water tanks;
- keep the party size and its noise to a minimum (4-10 is a manageable size for a group – mobile phones (unless used for navigation), portable radios etc. are not encouraged during the walk as full awareness is expected. These items are good for recreation at night in camp and for personal use a headphone;
- dispose of all rubbish and human wastes correctly - garbage should be carried out if possible;
- cross fences through gates or at a major post. At barbed-wire, one person will hold strands apart with a hand and boot whilst others pass through carefully. The last person through takes over this action for the first person;
- go around delicate vegetation, animal habitats, animal waterholes and fragile rock formations – not through them;
- avoid making campfires - use stoves if possible, or existing campfire sites. If a fire is made, make a small, correctly-constructed pit and restore the ground to its original condition after every ember has been extinguished;
- use soap and detergents <u>away</u> from water sources so that they are not polluted;
- use dead branches lifted up into prominent tree forks to blaze trails and rocks, dead timber or markings in soil to make signals rather than cutting marks into live

timber; and

- be polite to all whom you meet and thank those who have been of help.

13.4 Hygiene in Camp

Good hygiene is essential for keeping everyone in the party healthy and free of disease. Some basic ideas are:

- keep up a good standard of personal hygiene during the entire trip - wash the body (hands, face, under arms, inside of groin, waist), clean the teeth (even if it is just with a chewed twig), do the hair and keep clothing clean (especially socks) - get into and keep up a daily routine;
- A good personal kit may consist of a small sponge, soap, tooth brush, comb and small mirror in a rigid, sealable container as well as a small hand towel;
- keep garbage to a minimum and carry it out when you leave (if this is not possible, burn and bury deeply);
- site camps so that they are away from insects (have biodegradable repellent), other pests, poisonous plants, dangerous cliffs or holes, away from trees which may drop limbs and away from swamps and stagnant water;
- have a proper area for a latrine for camps more than one night. Even then it is advisable to make a proper latrine:
    - find a location well away from camp and water (at least 50 metres);
    - dig a steep-sided hole at least 50 cm. deep and about the same square near a convenient sapling

or stump for holding. Place the soil in a convenient heap nearby;

- two logs may be placed across the top of the hole as a seat (if needed) - sprinkle with cold ash from the fire to seal the timber and deter flies;
- use a large, broad leaf or bark as a cover to keep out flies;
- leave a can or small trowel (or flat stick) with which to shovel dirt to cover faeces after finishing;
- make a small track to the pit and mark with light-coloured stones or logs so that the way can be found at night (a candle in an inverted can with matches can also be left at the beginning of the track);
- toilet roll can be placed on a forked stick placed upright in the ground to keep the paper well off the ground. It can then be covered with a plastic bag in case of rain;
- a spare groundsheet can be wrapped around for some privacy; and
- it is most important to wash hands afterwards to stop infection - in areas with limited water, so have a bottle of hand sanitizer nearby.

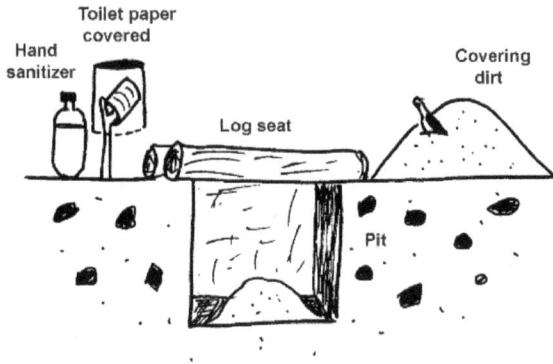

A complete bush latrine

Other useful hygiene matters include:
- do not use soap in a stream - wash away from the stream using minimum soap;
- discard waste water into a slops pit (a smaller pit just away from cam to be filled in later);
- keep open food away from insects and animals, either in a tightly-closed tent or in a closed pack kept under the fly. Keep foods in smaller, sealed containers and never leave exposed food nor food scraps lying around the camp; or
- in some countries with large scavengers (e.g. bears, wolves etc.), food may have to be kept away from camp in a strong bag positioned high up in a tree.

13.5 More on Walking –

The most important points about good, safe walking are that it should be done:

- in comfort;
- at a reasonable pace; and
- with perception of the track and surroundings.

Good boots and socks are most important. boots should support the ankles, give a good grip on the surface and be comfortable.

It is best to wear boots which have been worn-in. Wear new boots at home until they are soft, flexible and comfortable.

Maintain boots carefully, using polish everyday if they are leather (do not shine them too much, but keep a good layer of polish on. In wet conditions, add extra).

Socks should be kept soft and clean. Always have a clean pair ready (if not, turn used socks inside-out) and <u>never</u> wear wet socks if it can be helped.

Dry socks and boots naturally in the sun - do not dry them close to a fire (at night, move them well back if drying from a fire).

For general walking:

- walk at a natural pace with the arms slightly swinging for balance - carry the load of the pack by leaning slightly forward (but maintain upright posture if possible, with the pack <u>high</u> up on the back);
- going uphill, shorten the pace but lean forward slightly and keep the feet flat on the ground;

- going downhill, lengthen the stride leaning back slightly and go slowly. The knees will become painful so rest occasionally and stand upright;
- walking on **sloping sand** is best done slightly sideways by taking deliberate steps (checking that the sand will take the weight) and digging in the sides of the feet. Take great care of soft sand or white clay around the edges of pools or the sea. It may have a darker, wet look and appear to be hard. It may be quicksand and is to be avoided (if trapped in it, remove pack and breaststroke to the nearest hard support);
- in **soft snow** it is best if the group walks in single-file following in the leader's footsteps. when walking up a steep slope, dig the toes into the slope (even toe-kicking a step); going downhill (with great care), kick the heels deeply back into the snow to make a step. Look for lines of trees or rocks along which to walk. Watch out for a flat, vegetation-free strip which may indicate a stream hidden beneath the snow. Cross carefully at the narrowest point probing with a pole or go around. If the snow is too soft, make snowshoes from flexible, green branches and twine (one might have to back track to find these):

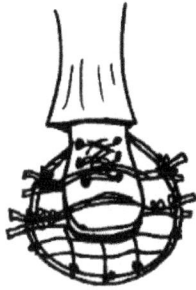

Bush Snowshoes

- always maintain a uniform pace but keep together. Walk at the pace of the slowest walker (to whom encouragement is positively given) and do not allow others to rush ahead;
- do not walk **at night** unless it cannot be helped. If so, try to keep to tracks and make the best use of light (moon or torches). Wait (about 30 min.) for night vision to adjust if using natural light and crouch down on occasions to silhouette the skyline or nearby water. Test each step carefully and stop regularly to check bearings. In a group, wear a light-coloured shirt or jacket or wear a white handkerchief pinned to the back; and
- **enjoy** the surroundings for that is what it is all about!

Chapter Fourteen: Other Useful Data

14.1 Conversions

The following conversions may be useful (approximations are given for simple calculations):

```
LENGTH:-  6 millimetres     = ¼ inch
         12 millimetres     = ½ inch
         25 millimetres     = 1 inch
        300 millimetres     = 12 inches
                            =1 foot
       1 metres (=1000 mm) = 39.39 inches
       1 kilometre (=1000 m) = 0.6 mile
       1.7 kilometres       = 1 mile
       5 kilometres         = 3 miles
    1000 kilometres         = 620 miles
  VOLUME
         5 millilitres      = 1 teaspoon
        20 millilitres      = 1 tablespoon
     140 millilitres   = ¼ pint
     250 millilitres   = 1 cup (small mug)
     300 millilitres   = 10 ounces
     560 millilitres   = 1 pint
     1 litre (1000 ml) = 1 quart
     4.5 litres        = 1 gallon
  MASS
     100 grams          =   3.5 ounces
     1 kilogram (1000 g) =   2.2 pounds (lbs)
                        (16 oz = 1 lb)
     1 litre of water weighs 1 kilogram
```

TEMPERATURE (degrees)
Water boils at normal air press at sea level at: 100^0 C
or 212^0 F

Converting Fahrenheit to Celsius:

Celsius = 5/9 (Fahrenheit – 32)
e.g. converting 212^0F to Celsius:

= 5/9 (212-32) = 5/9 (180)
= $\underline{5 \times 180}$ = 100^0 C
9

Converting Celsius to Fahrenheit:

Fahrenheit = (9/5 Celsius) + 32

e.g. converting 1000C to Fahrenheit:

= (9/5 x 100) + 32

$\underline{(9 \times 100)}$ + 32 = 180 +32 = 212^0F
5

100 C   Water boils   212 F

Temperature

Celsius		Fahrenheit
	40 ┼┼ 104	
30	┼┼ 86	Fahrenheit
C°	20 ┼┼ 68	F°
	10 ┼┼ 50	
	0 ┼┼ 32	Freezing Point
	-10 ┼┼ 14	
	-20 ┼┼ -4	
	-30 ┼┼ -22	
	-40 ┼┼ -40	

$$C = (F-32)\,5/9$$
$$F = (9/5 \times C) + 32$$

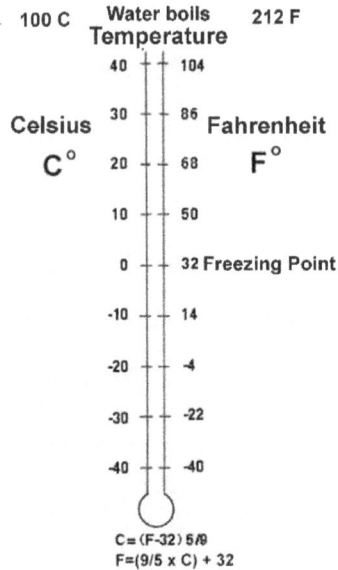

Wind chill factor – a very important hazard in cold, wet and windy conditions:

SPEED (km./hr.)					TEMPERATURE (0C)								
Calm	5	2	-1	-4	-7	-9	-12	-15	-18	-20	-23	-26	-29
8	1	-1	-4	-7	-9	-12	-15	-18	-20	-23	-26	-29	-32
16	-1	-7	-9	-12	-15	-18	-23	-26	-29	-32	-37	-40	-43
24	-4	-9	-12	-18	-20	-23	-29	-32	-34	-40	-43	-45	-51
32	-6	-12	-15	-18	-23	-26	-32	-34	-37	-43	-45	-51	-54
40	-9	-12	-18	-20	-26	-29	-34	-37	-43	-45	-51	-54	-59
48	-12	-15	-18	-23	-29	-32	-34	-40	-45	-48	-54	-57	-62
56	-12	-15	-20	-23	-29	-34	-37	-40	-45	-51	-54	-59	-62
64	-12	-18	-20	-26	-29	-34	-37	-43	-48	-51	-57	-59	-65

No Extra Effect above 64	LITTLE DANGER	INCREASING DANGER - FLESH MAY FREEZE IN 1 MINUTE	GREAT DANGER - FREEZING IN 30 SEC.

SPEED
1 kilometre/ hour = 0.3 metres/second
= 0.6 miles per hour
= 0.5 knots
1 mile per hour   = 1.6 km. per hour
= 0.9 knots
1 knot   = 1.8 km. per hour
= 1.1 miles per hour

Sound travels at 330 metres per second at sea level

14.2. Angles

1 circle = 360 degrees = 6400 mils
60 minutes of arc = 1 degree
60 seconds of arc = 1 minute of arc
1 hour of earth rotation = 15 degrees of
latitude

14.3 Trigonometry Ratios

Sometimes angles needed to be used in calculation trig. Rations such as

SINE	opposite/ hypotenuse
COSINE	adjacent/ hypotenuse
TANGENT	opposite/adjacent

This can be remembered by the ditty:
"**Old Harry Adams Has Old Apples**" for
SINE   COS   TAN   respectively
e.g. Sine = O/H   Cos = A/H   Tan = O/A

For the main angles of 30^0 45^0 60^0:

HYPOTENEUSE

OPPOSITE

90   angle θ

ADJACENT

45     $\sqrt{2}$

1

90   45

1

30   2

$\sqrt{3}$

90   60

1

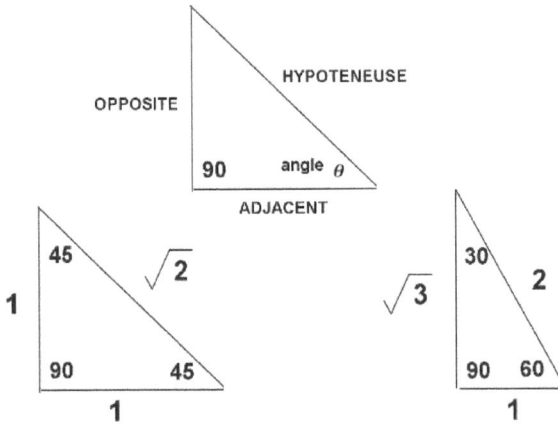

e.g. Sine of 30^0 = O/H = ½
Cosine of 30^0 = A/H = $\sqrt{3}$ / 2

Remember these triangles.

The main trig. values are:

θ	0°	30°	45°	60°	90°
sin θ	0	$\frac{1}{2}$	$\frac{\sqrt{2}}{2}$	$\frac{\sqrt{3}}{2}$	1
cos θ	1	$\frac{\sqrt{3}}{2}$	$\frac{\sqrt{2}}{2}$	$\frac{1}{2}$	0
tan θ	0	$\frac{\sqrt{3}}{3}$	1	$\sqrt{3}$	undef.

A set of Sine, Cosine and Tangent tables are given on following pages:

Table of sin (angle)

Angle	sin (a)	Angle	sin (a)	Angle	sin (a)	Angle	sin (a)
0.0	0.0	25.0	.4226	46.0	.7193	71.0	.9455
1.0	.0174	26.0	.4384	47.0	.7314	72.0	.9511
2.0	.0349	27.0	.4540	48.0	.7431	73.0	.9563
3.0	.0523	28.0	.4695	49.0	.7547	74.0	.9613
4.0	.0698	29.0	.4848	50.0	.7660	75.0	.9659
5.0	.0872	30.0	.5000	51.0	.7772	76.0	.9703
6.0	.1045	31.0	.5150	52.0	.7880	77.0	.9744
7.0	.1219	32.0	.5299	53.0	.7986	78.0	.9781
8.0	.1392	33.0	.5446	54.0	.8090	79.0	.9816
9.0	.1564	34.0	.5592	55.0	.8191	80.0	.9848
10.0	.1736	35.0	.5736	56.0	.8290	81.0	.9877
11.0	.1908	36.0	.5878	57.0	.8387	82.0	.9903
12.0	.2079	37.0	.6018	58.0	.8480	83.0	.9926
13.0	.2249	38.0	.6157	59.0	.8571	84.0	.9945
14.0	.2419	39.0	.6293	60.0	.8660	85.0	.9962
15.0	.2588	40.0	.6428	61.0	.8746	86.0	.9976
16.0	.2756	41.0	.6561	62.0	.8829	87.0	.9986
17.0	.2924	42.0	.6691	63.0	.8910	88.0	.9994
18.0	.3090	43.0	.6820	64.0	.8988	89.0	.9998
19.0	.3256	44.0	.6947	65.0	.9063	90.0	1.00
20.0	.3420	45.0	.7071	66.0	.9135		
21.0	.3584			67.0	.9205		
22.0	.3746			68.0	.9272		
23.0	.3907			69.0	.9336		
24.0	.4067			70.0	.9397		

Table of cos(angle)

Angle	cos(a)	Angle	cos(a)	Angle	cos(a)	Angle	cos(a)
0.0	1.00	25.0	.9063	46.0	.6947	71.0	.3256
1.0	.9998	26.0	.8988	47.0	.6820	72.0	.3090
2.0	.9994	27.0	.8910	48.0	.6691	73.0	.2924
3.0	.9986	28.0	.8829	49.0	.6561	74.0	.2756
4.0	.9976	29.0	.8746	50.0	.6428	75.0	.2588
5.0	.9962	30.0	.8660	51.0	.6293	76.0	.2419
6.0	.9945	31.0	.8571	52.0	.6157	77.0	.2249
7.0	.9926	32.0	.8480	53.0	.6018	78.0	.2079
8.0	.9903	33.0	.8387	54.0	.5878	79.0	.1908
9.0	.9877	34.0	.8290	55.0	.5736	80.0	.1736
10.0	.9848	35.0	.8191	56.0	.5592	81.0	.1564
11.0	.9816	36.0	.8090	57.0	.5446	82.0	.1392
12.0	.9781	37.0	.7986	58.0	.5299	83.0	.1219
13.0	.9744	38.0	.7880	59.0	.5150	84.0	.1045
14.0	.9703	39.0	.7772	60.0	.5000	85.0	.0872
15.0	.9659	40.0	.7660	61.0	.4848	86.0	.0698
16.0	.9613	41.0	.7547	62.0	.4695	87.0	.0523
17.0	.9563	42.0	.7431	63.0	.4540	88.0	.0349
18.0	.9511	43.0	.7314	64.0	.4384	89.0	.0174
19.0	.9455	44.0	.7193	65.0	.4226	90.0	0.0
20.0	.9397	45.0	.7071	66.0	.4067		
21.0	.9336			67.0	.3907		
22.0	.9272			68.0	.3746		
23.0	.9205			69.0	.3584		
24.0	.9135			70.0	.3420		

Table of tan(angle)

Angle	tan(a)	Angle	tan(a)	Angle	tan(a)	Angle	tan(a)
0.0	0.00	25.0	.4663	46.0	1.0355	71.0	2.9042
1.0	.0175	26.0	.4877	47.0	1.0724	72.0	3.0777
2.0	.0349	27.0	.5095	48.0	1.1106	73.0	3.2709
3.0	.0524	28.0	.5317	49.0	1.1504	74.0	3.4874
4.0	.0699	29.0	.5543	50.0	1.1918	75.0	3.7321
5.0	.0875	30.0	.5773	51.0	1.2349	76.0	4.0108
6.0	.1051	31.0	.6009	52.0	1.2799	77.0	4.3315
7.0	.1228	32.0	.6249	53.0	1.3270	78.0	4.7046
8.0	.1405	33.0	.6494	54.0	1.3764	79.0	5.1446
9.0	.1584	34.0	.6745	55.0	1.4281	80.0	5.6713
10.0	.1763	35.0	.7002	56.0	1.4826	81.0	6.3138
11.0	.1944	36.0	.7265	57.0	1.5399	82.0	7.1154
12.0	.2126	37.0	.7535	58.0	1.6003	83.0	8.1443
13.0	.2309	38.0	.7813	59.0	1.6643	84.0	9.5144
14.0	.2493	39.0	.8098	60.0	1.7321	85.0	11.430
15.0	.2679	40.0	.8391	61.0	1.8040	86.0	14.301
16.0	.2867	41.0	.8693	62.0	1.8907	87.0	19.081
17.0	.3057	42.0	.9004	63.0	1.9626	88.0	28.636
18.0	.3249	43.0	.9325	64.0	2.0503	89.0	57.290
19.0	.3443	44.0	.9657	65.0	2.1445	90.0	infinite
20.0	.3640	45.0	1.000	66.0	2.2460		
21.0	.3839			67.0	2.3559		
22.0	.4040			68.0	2.4751		
23.0	.4245			69.0	2.6051		
24.0	.4452			70.0	2.7475		

Remember: Pythagoras' Theorem states that:

$(\text{hypotenuse})^2 = (\text{opposite}^2) + (\text{adjacent}^2)$

Some useful square roots are:

$\sqrt{2} = 1.414$ $\sqrt{3} = 1.732$ $\sqrt{5} = 2.236$ $\sqrt{6} = 2.449$
$\sqrt{7} = 2.648$ $\sqrt{8} = 2.828$ $\sqrt{10} = 3.162$

Other square roots can be found by **approximation**, i.e. thinking of a number that if SQUARED will approximate that number.

e.g. consider $\sqrt{68}$:

Now $8^2 = 64$ which is only just less than 68, so try $(8.2)^2 = 67.24$, still just short so try $(8.25)^2 = 68.06$. Close enough for practical purposes.

About the Author

Dr. Scott on the Franz Josef Glacier, New Zealand

Dr. Peter Terence Scott was born in Sydney, Australia and had a professional teaching career spanning over forty years. As a schoolboy and well into adult life, he was an active caver, hiker, climber and skier, becoming an Honorary State ranger and a trip leader in the Duke of Edinburgh Scheme. He studied at university part time and obtained a Bachelor of Science degree in Geology, a Masters' Degrees in Exploration Geology and Educational Administration and later a Doctorate in Education. During this time, he also trained as an Army Reservist and was commissioned into the Infantry as a Platoon Commander. After eight years in the Army, he switched uniforms and became an Officer/Instructor in the Naval Cadets and commanded one of their training ships as well as having six training cruises aboard Tall Ships along the eastern Australian coast. He has travelled to many of the wilderness places of all six continents including the high Andes, North American Rockies, the Swiss Alps, the Amazon Jungle, the Antarctic Peninsula and the deserts of North Africa to name a few. He is the author of over twenty books including those listed here.

Other Books by the Author

FICTION

Letters from San Rafael (as Hernan Moreno Ruiz). Set in South America in the 1880's, this is a collection of letters smuggled home by Don Hernan Moreno, an Intelligence officer of the Peruvian Army who has been captured by the Ecuadorans during a border dispute. Taken to the fortified hacienda in Banos, in the mountains of Ecudor, he and his sargeant, Garcia, are treated as honoured guests. Each of the ten stories tells of the life and times of people in the hacienda and beyond. The final chapter is the climax of the entire book.

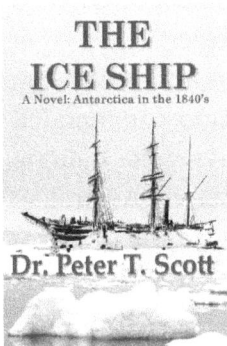

The Ice Ship. Set mainly in the Antarctic in the 1840's, this is the story of the survival of the crew of the futuristic auxiliary steam whaler, the AUSTRALIS which has become trapped in the ice following its voyage south along the Antarctic Peninsula. Based upon actual observations and experience of the author during a 2011 voyage into the same region on a small ex-research vessel.

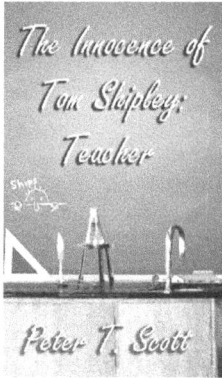

A humorous look at a young teacher's introduction to teaching as a 19-year-old Acting Head of Science in a new school and his coming of age. Full of a host of characters from both the staff and student bodies with many funny events based upon the author's 44-year teaching career.

NON-FICTION

Adventures in Earth Science is an in-depth, traditional Earth Science textbook on Geology, Meteorology, Oceanography and Astronomy. The latest scientific information has been given in the text including chapters on climate change and the future use of fuels and energy. The book contains over 700 pages, 1200 photographs and illustrations mostly taken by the author. It also includes 32 video links taken by the author to explain various skills as well as excursions to many exotic places in support of the text. Also has companion **Teachers' Guide** and **Laboratory Manual**.

The contents of this book have also been rearranged into the **Adventures in Earth Science Series** of eight smaller individual books in both electronic and A5 print editions.

| Exploration Science | Fossils- Life in the Rocks | Riches from the Earth | A Dangerous Planet: Volcanoes & Earthquakes |

| Rocks - Building The Earth | Changing the Surface: Weathering and Erosion | Through Sea and Sky: Oceanography and Meteorology | Beyond Planet Earth: Astronomy |

Adventures in Earth and Environmental Science is a two-volume textbook on the environment, how it is monitored and implications for the future. They come in electronic format and as A4-sized print editions with a **Laboratory Manual** for each volume and a **Teachers' Guide**.

263

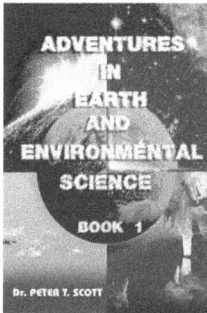

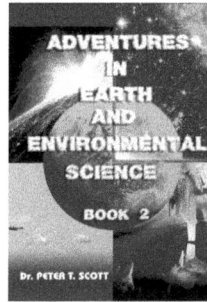

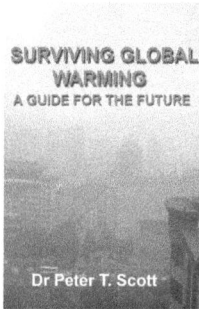

Surviving Global Warming - A Guide for the Future is a comprehensive explanation of the natural and man-made causes of global warming with data from a wide range of reputable scientific bodies such as CSIRO and NASA. Written with many innovative suggestions for coping with the consequences of future global warming at the home, local and government levels. It comes as an electronic or printed edition.

All of these books are available in electronic format for any PC or tablet in Kindle format which can be read on any device using the free Kindle App. Or as print editions. Available at all Internet book outlets or from **Felix Publishing** by contacting them at:

info.felixpublishing@gmail.com